GRACE ENJOYED

Delighting in our God in the ordinary moments of life

100 DEVOTIONS FOR WOMEN

JUDIE PUCKETT

STORIED
publishing

Copyright © 2023 Judie Puckett

All rights reserved.

No part of this book may be reproduced in any form or by any electronic or mechanical means, including information storage and retrieval systems, without written permission from the author, except for the use of brief quotations in a book review.

Unless otherwise indicated, Scripture quotations are from the ESV Bible (The Holy Bible, English Standard Version), copyright 2001 by Crossway, a publishing ministry of Good News Publishers. 2011 Text Edition. All rights reserved.

ISBN: 978-1-951991-39-5

Edited by Doug Serven

Cover design by Sean Benesh

Published by Storied Publishing

IN PRAISE OF GRACE ENJOYED

Someone has said that all of life illustrates Biblical truth. Judie Puckett's book, *Grace Enjoyed*, takes what is ordinary, and with profound insight, makes it stand up and sing "The Hallelujah Chorus." In a fun and delightful way, the ordinary things of life become the window through which I could see God. I know this is a book of devotions for women, but this guy was blessed, inspired, and encouraged. If you're a guy, give this book to the women in your life, but, be sure and read it for yourself.
Steve Brown
Seminary professor, author, and broadcaster
Key Life Ministries

If you are hungry for God's Word to be applied practically and accurately in an accessible devotional, look no further. Judie has put together a delightful collection of easy-to-read but hard-to-forget devotions that will challenge and encourage you. With Biblical insight and helpful illustrations, you will walk away from these readings remembering God's Word.
Christine Gordon
Co-founder, At His Feet Studies
Author

I have had the privilege of seeing Judie's commitment to the Gospel enable women to flourish in her community. These devotions make up a Gospel mosaic, affirming for us what is most true about those of us whose lives are hidden in Christ. With the truth and eternal beauty of God's Word, Judie names our struggles while pointing to our hope. This collection of devotions stirs up our affections for the Lord by centering our vision on his steadfast love for us. These accessible portraits of God will encourage you to press forward in faith, increase your joy, expand your wisdom, and clarify your sense of calling, identity, and belonging to the Living God whose love for you is never-ending.

Meaghan May
Elders' Wives Liaison, Presbyterian Church in America (PCA) Women's Ministry Director, Covenant Church of Naples Trainer, Parakaleo

These are precious reflections of grace that not only feed the soul but empower us toward God's mission. I'm so grateful for the gift Judie is to the church and to the many women who benefit from her ministry!

Lloyd Kim
Coordinator, Mission to the World

"A word fitly spoken is like apples of gold in a setting of silver" (Proverbs 25:11). Messages suitable to the occasion are precious because they provide what we need to persevere with hope in a broken world. Judie Puckett has given us 100 such messages in *Grace Enjoyed: Delighting in our God in the Ordinary Moments of Life*. Even though she's addressing it to women, I'm claiming them for myself too! Thank you, sister, for helping us to find joy in the ordinary.

Irwyn L. Ince, Jr.
Coordinator, Mission to North America
Author, *The Beautiful Community*

In her devotional, *Grace Enjoyed*, Judie Puckett winsomely speaks the truth of the Gospel into the joys and sorrows of our daily lives. Judie invites us into her life, sharing real stories that we all can relate to, reminding us that we are not alone. Reading this devotional is like sitting with a good friend sipping a cup of tea, sharing our stories, and pointing each other to Jesus. Judie points us to God's Word, profoundly showing how Jesus meets us in these ordinary moments of our lives. She reminds us that we all have a story to tell, a story of God's provision and faithfulness, a story of our Savior's love and forgiveness, a story of hope.

Cheryl Mullis
Director of Adult Ministries, Evangelical Presbyterian Church of Annapolis
Northeast Regional Advisor, PCA Women's National Team

For several years now, I have had the privilege of working alongside Judie, who directs our Women's Ministries. The compassionate spirit that she exhibits every day in serving Christ at Chapelgate and the tender care she has engendered into her ministry are fully on display in *Grace Enjoyed*. What she writes, she does. What she says, she embodies. This is a beautiful devotional.

Mike Khandjian
Pastor, Chapelgate Presbyterian Church
Author, *A Sometimes Stumbling Life*

Judie Puckett's *Grace Enjoyed* is rich in grace, brimming with hope, and grounded in the goodness and sovereignty of God. Puckett uses clear, well-written chapters and every-day anecdotes (dirty dishes, imitation crab meat, swim floaties) to point readers back to the Gospel. She invites us to recenter our lives on Christ in the midst of the mundane. Don't be fooled by the bite-sized chapters; *Grace Enjoyed* is worth savoring.

Maria Garriott
Director, Baltimore Antioch Leadership Movement
Author, *Stronger Together* and *A Thousand Resurrections*

What is the point of having a God of grace if we don't enjoy the grace he's given? In her devotional book, *Grace Enjoyed*, Judie Puckett leads her readers to refreshing wells of God's word. This 100-day devotional is simple in organization but complex in revealing our heart's constant reluctance to accept the grace of God

in our lives. Judie can weave stories with imaginative language and imagery to get the readers to gaze at the glory of God. I am thankful for her vulnerability but, more importantly, her poignant message that I need to be reminded of—that God delights in us!
Andy Lewis
Lead Teaching Pastor, Mitchell Road Presbyterian Church

Judie Puckett offers women very practical advice in facing the ordinary struggles of daily life. In each instance, she clearly points us to Jesus and to his Word, reminding her readers that we are never alone as we experience the trials in this broken world.
Pam Benton

Judie Puckett's new book is delightful, engaging, and helpful. *Grace Enjoyed* proves to be a good friend to its readers because Judie reminds them that God is near with his caring presence. Each meditation awakens the heart to God's presence in the exact times that we are most prone to forget His sustaining grace—the ordinary, unspectacular, ho-hum moments of our everyday lives. I will give this devotion first to my wife and then to the ladies of our congregation.
Brian Smith
Pastor, Calvary Assembly of God

Puckett's ability to connect everyday stories with deep biblical truth is captivating. Each devotional offers the clear hope of Jesus in the face of our very human needs. It is full of rich theology and Christ-centered biblical application while being easily approachable. I highly recommend this book for anyone looking to encounter God in the ordinary of life.
Dan Passerelli
President, Metro Baltimore Seminary

Judie's devotions encourage us to see the unchanging character of

God as revealed in Scripture, which is much needed when life is ever-changing. In each short story, she helps us see Jesus as the center of God's glorious redemption story and the wondrous grace we have within it. This book helps women to set their minds on things above when things on earth are clamoring for our attention. What a treasure trove.

Lauri Hogle
Founder, Singing Christ's Hope

The art of writing a devotional is a true gift. Judie exemplifies a woman whom God has called to bless you with that gift. Judie pulls out what may seem basic and invites the reader into a deeper look at their mind, soul, and heart and ultimately into a deeper connection with God. As the title states, *Grace Enjoyed* encompasses each writing as we are reminded of the grace that God so freely gives us. I am honored to call Judie a friend and sister in Christ.

Laura Starsoneck
Author, *Single-Handedly Blessed*

Puckett's devotional offers women a resource that is personal, accessible, and theologically grounded. Drawing from her own walk with Jesus, Puckett invites the reader to come near to Jesus and apply the transforming power of the Gospel to her own heart and life in 100 different ways. I highly recommend this resource to any woman looking to deepen and strengthen her relationship with Christ.

Jeff McMullen
Executive Director, Life Counseling Center

This devotional is gold. Judie takes life's mundane moments and finds redeeming threads that show us more of who our God is. Big theological concepts, like our union with Christ, become as simple to understand as making a cup of coffee. I am excited to share this devotional with every woman that I know who desires that her days have an eternal impact.

Jane Anne Wilson
Advisor on the PCA Permanent Committee for Discipleship Ministries,
Former Northeast Regional Advisor for PCA Women's Ministry

CONTENTS

Dedication — xiii

1. First Things First — 1
2. Unbroken Resolution — 3
3. Washed Away Seeds — 5
4. Identity Crisis — 7
5. Interruptions — 9
6. God Gives the Growth — 11
7. Baseball — 13
8. Jump in the water! — 15
9. A Mother's Heart — 17
10. A New Name — 19
11. Personal Words — 21
12. Dirty Dishes — 23
13. Inseparable — 25
14. Go-To Stories — 27
15. Fierce Protector — 30
16. Ambassadors — 32
17. Looking Back — 35
18. He Makes All Things Beautiful — 38
19. Home — 40
20. Unparalleled Power — 42
21. Trust God — 44
22. Gus — 46
23. Don't Be Fooled — 48
24. The Judge — 51
25. Where Are the Weapons? — 54
26. Collected Tears — 56
27. Building History — 58
28. Hidden — 60
29. Cheering for You — 62
30. Satisfy Us — 64

31. Safe, Loved, and Not Alone	67
32. The House of the Lord	70
33. Trust the Floaties	72
34. Exposing Sin	74
35. Fighting Fear	76
36. Character Is Everything	78
37. Met with Kindness	81
38. Hidden Treasure	83
39. Pride before a Fall	85
40. Smart Cars	87
41. The Expert	90
42. Even Disobedience?	93
43. Road Signs	95
44. God Comes Running	97
45. God's Masterpiece	100
46. Just Start	102
47. Dog Hair	104
48. Meant to be Shared	106
49. Deeply Moved	108
50. Air Fryers	111
51. Everyone Is Looking for You	113
52. The Rescuer	115
53. Can't Keep It In!	117
54. Coming For You	120
55. Called into Existence	122
56. Lessons from Golf	125
57. Make Us Faithful	127
58. Pull the Weeds	129
59. Just a Word	132
60. Building a Grateful Heart	134
61. His Desire	137
62. Kindness & Repentance	140
63. Face to Face	143
64. Becoming Your Parent	145
65. Come Out of Hiding	147
66. Building a Kingdom	149
67. He Gives More	152

68. Imitation Crab Meat		155
69. Just Get Here		157
70. Front Row Seats		160
71. Contagious Worship		163
72. Front Porch Presents		165
73. Still Invited		167
74. It All Ends Well		169
75. The Story's Author		171
76. Tennis Shoes		174
77. One Word Changes Everything		177
78. Hey Babe!		179
79. Fulfilling a Purpose		182
80. I Got Adopted! I Got Adopted!		184
81. Well-Proved		186
82. Surgery		188
83. Trust the Process		191
84. A Glimpse Inside		194
85. Bread Trucks and Benefits		197
86. The Fence		199
87. Remember & Retell		201
88. Dogs		204
89. Unity		207
90. Firefighters		210
91. Stubbed Toes		212
92. Secret Things		214
93. 5 More Pounds		217
94. Finish Lines		219
95. One for the Many		221
96. Kintsugi		224
97. A Lifetime of Unlearning		226
98. I Need a Little Christmas		229
99. Joy and Sorrow		232
100. Not a Hallmark Movie		234
About the Author		237
About White BlackBird Books		239
Also by White Blackbird Books		241

DEDICATION

To Aaron, my husband, best friend, and partner in all things—This book never would have happened without you. Thank you for believing in me far more than I believe in myself. I love you.

To Annabelle, Abe, and Micah—You are our greatest joy! May the Lord always direct your hearts to the love of God and the steadfastness of Christ.

To Mom, the Master Proofreader—Thank you for the countless hours you spent reading and rereading these pages. You are amazing, and I love you!

To the Women of Chapelgate, for whom these devotions were originally written—You are so dear to me! Thank you for your faithful love and encouragement.

To my pastor and friend, Mike—Your support and excitement for this project, especially in the final stages, overwhelms me. Thank you!

Chapter One
FIRST THINGS FIRST

We love because he first loved us.
1 John 4:19

When one of my children was young and first learning how to toast a bagel, he asked me, "Mom, do I toast the bagel first and then put on the cream cheese or do I put the cream cheese on first and then toast the bagel?" I was so relieved he asked! What a mess (and a smell) he would have created if the cream cheese went on before toasting! When operating a toaster, order really matters.

In the Christian life, when it comes to understanding faith and works, order matters too. Perhaps we confuse it sometimes because it is so contrary to the way our world works. In the business world, if you work hard, you earn a promotion. In the exercise and fitness world, if you put forth enough effort, you reap the rewards of strong muscles and healthy lungs. Even in relationships, you often reap what you sow.

But, in the economy of the Gospel, the opposite is true. You cannot earn God's favor and love by your effort, hard work, or determination. When it comes to your salvation and your standing with God, your merit or performance will not secure his devotion to you. Before the foundation of the world, God decided to set his love and affection on you: *"We love because he first loved us"* (1 John 4:19). He chose us; we did not choose him (Romans 3:10–12). It is from the place of being a beloved child of God that we love God and surrender our lives to Him. Because you are his, because he has called you his treasured possession, your faith produces good works.

So why does this matter? Why is it important that we get the order right? It matters because everything we do flows out of the motivation of our hearts. If we believe that we must earn God's love and favor, then we will end up in either a pool of pride or a well of despair. If we believe that God's affection is conditioned upon our obedience, then we will be driven by duty and not delight.

The Father loves you. He delights in you. He is glad that you are his. Let that truth sink deep into your soul today. You are, for sure, called to good works. You are called to obey. You are called to lay down your life for others. But, first, you are called to know that you are his, that he loves you, and that he has forever committed himself to you. From that place, go and do. First, sit and be warmed by the affection of your Father. Then, go out.

Sister, toast the bagel first.

Chapter Two

UNBROKEN RESOLUTION

> *And I am sure of this, that he who began a good work in you will bring it to completion at the day of Jesus Christ.*
> Philippians 1:6

I bet you can easily guess what these three things have in common: exercise more, eat healthy, and save money.

These are among the top New Year's resolutions every year. Gyms are packed in January. Budgets are set. Grocery lists include lots of vegetables and forbid junk food. At the start of the new year, we are optimistically motivated and absolutely determined to remain consistent in our resolve. New beginnings are wonderful.

However, it is rare that a determined resolution in January continues through December. Motivation wanes, and former habits resurface before spring blooms. Have you been there? Failure to accomplish our goals is discouraging; guilt creeps into our hearts.

The Scriptures, however, bring good news to our hearts. ***For***

what God has resolved to accomplish in you, he absolutely, without fail, will complete! His determination will never waver. His power always achieves what his will desires. He never ever fails to fulfill what he promises. Never! Be encouraged today! This is true for YOU!

So make those resolutions if you choose. Set goals. Work hard. Steward your body well.

But when failure comes (and it will; it always does), be reminded that there is One who never fails. The purposes that God sets for you will be fulfilled because he is faithful. So today if you are stuck in despair and failure, remember your God. What he has started, he will finish. Fix your eyes on him. He is faithful.

Chapter Three
WASHED AWAY SEEDS

> *Your kingdom is an everlasting kingdom, and your dominion endures throughout all generations. The Lord is faithful in all his words and kind in all his works.*
> Psalm 145:13

Two weeks ago, my husband spent an entire day reseeding part of our pasture. A large section had been regraded the previous fall and there sat a huge rectangle of wet dirt where grass needed to be planted. He walked back and forth and back and forth in ankle-deep mud for hours sowing the seeds. After the scattering, he went back and forth and back and forth again, through the mud, laying straw over the fragile seeds to protect the tiny plants. Because of the laborious and time-consuming effort, he went to bed sore, sunburned, and exhausted.

Two nights later, it stormed. Really stormed. Hard rain and lots of it. Every time it rains like that on the farm, a small river runs through the pasture down to the pond. This was no exception. Much of the seed washed away. When I woke up the morning after the flooding and saw that stream of water, all I could think was how all that work was for nothing. Then, I remembered the providence of God.

Sometimes we see his sovereign ruling hand at work, and it makes sense, and it is beautiful. But sometimes we see his reigning hand at work and it doesn't make sense, and it sure doesn't look beautiful. So, what do we do in those moments? Where do we go when our circumstances don't seem to line up with who we think God is? Where do we go when hours of hard work and energy seem to just get washed away?

Sisters, in those times, we must run to his Word. The Scriptures are our confidence and our hope! We remember that God's control is perfect and absolute. We remember that his ways are always good, and his character is always kind.

> *Your kingdom is an everlasting kingdom,*
> *and your dominion endures throughout all generations.*
> ***The Lord is faithful in all his words***
> ***and kind in all his works.***
> *The Lord upholds all who are falling*
> *and raises up all who are bowed down.*
> *The eyes of all look to you,*
> *and you give them their food in due season.*
> *You open your hand;*
> *you satisfy the desire of every living thing.*
> ***The Lord is righteous in all his ways***
> ***and kind in all his works.***
> (Psalm 145:13–17)

When life's circumstances seem to contradict what you know is true, go to God's Word. Submerse yourself in it. Trust him. He is always kind and always good.

Chapter Four
IDENTITY CRISIS

And David said to the men who stood by him, "What shall be done for the man who kills this Philistine and takes away the reproach from Israel? For who is this uncircumcised Philistine, that he should defy the armies of the living God?"
1 Samuel 17:26

An identity crisis can strike anyone. A loss of a job causes you to rethink your identity. Relational fractures make you question your self-worth. Your kids grow up and you wonder what's out there other than motherhood. Mid-life hits,  and it shakes your security. Marital status has defined you for so long that you wonder if it really constitutes the sum total of your identity. Sister, no one is immune to the doubt that surrounds our understanding of who we are.

But the good news is this—these identity crises are not new, and God offers us hope in the midst of them.

The story of David and Goliath is familiar to most of us. Even people who have never opened a Bible are often acquainted with this tale of the young shepherd boy who defeated the well-armored Philistine giant. While this story predominantly points us to the power and goodness of God, it also speaks about an identity crisis.

In the account recorded in 1 Samuel 17, the Philistine warrior, Goliath, stands on the mountain and taunts the people of God, daring them to send a man to fight him. No one in Israel could compare with Goliath in size or strength; so, they cower in fear. We read:

> *He [Goliath] stood and shouted to the ranks of Israel, "Why have you come out to draw up for battle? Am I not a Philistine, and are you not servants of Saul? Choose a man for yourselves, and let him come down to me."* (1 Samuel 17:8)

Did you catch the crisis? Goliath identified the people of Israel as **servants of Saul, and they believe it**. As such, they hid in fear and despaired. They forgot who they were.

You see, Israel was not to be identified as the servants of Saul! That was NOT their identity. They were God's chosen treasured possession, a people holy to the Lord (Deuteronomy 7:6). They were the army of the Living God (1 Samuel 17:26)!

And when David comes onto the scene a few verses later, he reminds them of that (17:26, 36). They are the army of the Living God! The young shepherd remembered his true identity. David's confidence in facing Goliath did not come because he was a valiant warrior, but because he knew and trusted his God. He knew the One to whom he belonged and that changed everything.

The same is true for us, friends. You belong to the One who has sacrificed his life to make you his very own. Your life is hidden with him now (Colossians 3:3) and that changes everything. You can trust, not in your own strength or your self-made identity, but rather in the God who treasures you.

Chapter Five
INTERRUPTIONS

*The heart of man plans his way,
but the LORD establishes his steps.*
Proverbs 16:9

Recently, a friend arrived at a meeting at church and realized that she had forgotten her phone. Despite the inconvenience for her to run home again, she had no choice. Frustrated, she knew she needed to have her phone with her for the day and would be unable to go home later. Annoyed, she turned around and went home.

When she returned to the church, now late at this point, she noticed a woman who seemed to be lost, wandering from door to door near the entrance to the building. She could have just rushed past; she was late after all. But she didn't.

She kindly asked the lost stranger if she needed help. With broken English, the timid woman quietly replied that she was looking for the ESL group. My friend quickly responded, "That's where I'm heading! I'll be happy to take you there."

As she recounted this story, she said, "I think if I hadn't asked her what she was looking for, she would've just left." And if she hadn't left her phone at home, she would've arrived on time and never met this precious woman wandering outside the church doors.

Sometimes the inconveniences of our days can be frustrating. Sometimes the interruptions really mess up our to-do list. But sometimes those interruptions are God-ordained moments. In Mark 5, we read the story of Jesus on his way to heal the daughter of a man named Jairus. An important ruler of the day, Jairus had a big crisis on his hands. Because his daughter is near death, he needs Jesus to come with him NOW and save her life.

This is an urgent moment for Jesus and his disciples! However, as they head that way, the journey is interrupted. A woman who has an issue of blood touches Jesus' garment. Instantly she is cured, and the Healer knows it.

But here's a fantastic part of the story—Jesus stops. In the middle of his very important agenda, he stops to talk to her. I can imagine if I had been one of the disciples (or Jairus), I would've been thinking, "We really don't have time for this, Jesus! Let's go. We have an emergency to deal with." But Jesus stops. In that moment, ***the interruption is the calling.***

It's easy for us to get so caught up in what we have on our calendars for the day that interruptions are seen as major inconveniences. But if we believe that God is sovereign over even the interruptions of our well-planned days, then even those "unplanned" moments are opportunities for us to see his hand and his goodness in our lives. Today, when your day doesn't go exactly as you intend, embrace God's sovereign rule, and expect that his good and loving hand has ordained this interruption for you.

Chapter Six
GOD GIVES THE GROWTH

What then is Apollos? What is Paul? Servants through whom you believed, as the Lord assigned to each. ***I planted, Apollos watered, but God gave the growth****. So, neither he who plants nor he who waters is anything, but only God who gives the growth. He who plants and he who waters are one, and each will receive his wages according to his labor. For we are God's fellow workers. You are God's field, God's building. According to God's grace given to me, like a skilled master builder I laid a foundation and someone else is building on it. Let each one take care how he builds upon it.*
1 Corinthians 3:5–10

Last summer, a high school youth group traveled to a Latin American country to serve with a sister church. While there, part of the group worked to enclose an open outdoor space and build a room that would be used for Sunday  morning classes. From power-washing the floor, to measuring and sawing boards, to framing walls, these young people labored resolutely in the very hot Central American sun. However, despite their amazing efforts, they did not complete the project.

But here's the cool thing—that is exactly the way it was supposed to be! One of the pastors of the sister church actually did NOT want the American team to finish. Rather, it was important to him that his church also contribute to the building effort. His people needed to be personally invested in the construction of that space. But even more than that, he longed for his congregation to see the Body of Christ (from various parts of the world) work together to build the Kingdom of Christ. This was far more valuable that the mere completion of a construction project.

While one team laid a foundation, another team would build on it. What some of God's people started, others would finish.

The same is true for us. As we embrace the role that God has given us to play in building his Kingdom, we recognize that we may not see the fruit of our labors right now. Perhaps we plant small seeds of the Gospel in the heart of a co-worker. Maybe we offer forgiveness to a family member who has repeatedly wounded us. Perhaps we welcome a neighbor with the love and warmth of God's love. We may not be having long in-depth conversations about redemption, but as God gives us opportunities, we testify to the love of Christ. We are laying a foundation. We may not see any fruit, but we trust the Master Gardener. We believe that each of us has a part to play in building God's Kingdom, and no part is too small.

So, wherever you are today, remember you are a member of a huge family and a glorious kingdom. You have a very specific role to play, even if you have yet to see the fruit of your labor. So, go and plant seeds and trust. Trust the Master. He will bring the growth.

Chapter Seven
BASEBALL

Then I saw a new heaven and a new earth, for the first heaven and the first earth had passed away, and the sea was no more. And I saw the holy city, new Jerusalem, coming down out of heaven from God, prepared as a bride adorned for her husband. And I heard a loud voice from the throne saying, "Behold, the dwelling place of God is with man. He will dwell with them, and they will be his people, and God himself will be with them as their God. He will wipe away every tear from their eyes, and death shall be no more, neither shall there be mourning, nor crying, nor pain anymore, for the former things have passed away.
Revelation 21:1–4

Both of my sons play baseball, and I love watching them. I really enjoy spending sunny afternoons on the ball field; but I sometimes get anxious when one of them steps to the plate with two outs and the  tying run stands on third. My hands get a little sweaty. When one of them pitches and struggles to find the strike zone, my stomach ties in knots. I feel pretty nervous and troubled as I watch.

I recently watched a video from one of their games. But I

wasn't anxious at all because I knew the end of the story; I knew how the game turned out. The fear of the unknown disappeared. I could still experience the joy of a triple down the right-field line, and it still felt like a punch in the gut when my shortstop made an error. But instead of anxiety; I felt peace even when I watched a misplayed ground ball.

The same can be true about life for Christ-followers. While life is full of joy and sorrow and we experience the full gamut of those emotions, we know how the Story finishes, and that changes everything! In the end, all will be made right. In the end, the Good Guy wins. In the end, there will be no more tears.

That doesn't mean that we don't grieve the sorrows that living in a broken world brings. We absolutely do. It also doesn't mean that we don't enjoy the blessings of the day; we do! God has given us everything richly to enjoy (1 Timothy 6:17). It means that Christ offers us a peace that comes from knowing that he is sovereignly directing all of creation toward a very good end! We are free to rest in the powerful words of Jesus: ***"I have said these things to you, that in me you may have peace. In the world you will have tribulation. But take heart; I have overcome the world"*** (John 16:33).

Friends, we know the end of the Story! While this world is full of both joy and pain, high highs and really low lows, in the midst of it, the One who holds it all together offers us his peace. The type of peace that passes all understanding. Today, whether your heart is light and free, or you carry unspeakable burdens, he has overcome the world! Take heart in the assurance that a better day will be here soon. The happy ending is written.

Chapter Eight

JUMP IN THE WATER!

But for me it is good to be near God; I have made the Lord God my refuge, that I may tell of all your works.
Psalm 73:28

With warm air and sunshine, spending an afternoon on the water in a boat can be a wonderful experience. But when calm waters become choppy, a delightful afternoon changes into the worst day. While the bobbing of the boat may rock some to sleep, for others, the constant swaying and bouncing on the water causes dizziness, sweaty palms, and unbearable nausea.

Being seasick must be one of the worst sensations in the world! But they say (you know the famous "they") that if you feel seasick and you can do it safely—jump in the water. Almost immediately, the symptoms subside, and you feel much better. Apparently, when your brain merges the motions it feels with what you see, relief follows. If you change your environment, everything changes.

The incredibly raw and relatable Psalm 73 speaks to this. The singer struggles in this psalm. He says that his feet had almost slipped (v. 2). Everywhere he looks, it seems that the wicked prosper. The arrogant seem to get everything they want with no consequence. Clothed with pride, they oppress. The psalmist can't make sense of how the wicked are, *"...always at ease, they increase in riches"* (v. 12). They even mock God. He goes on to say, *"All in vain have I kept my heart clean and washed my hands in innocence"* (v. 13). Discouraged and frustrated, he can't fathom why things go how they go. He does not understand and feels weary and frustrated.

Can you relate? Do you look around and wonder why what is right seems wrong and the wrong gets declared right? Are you frustrated that the wicked seem to prosper? Does life seem wildly out of balance to you? If so, you are in good company.

Thankfully, the psalmist doesn't leave us stuck in frustration and despair. He writes, *"But when I thought how to understand this, it seemed to me a wearisome task,* **until I went into the sanctuary of God;** *then I discerned their end"* (vv. 16–17).

Did you catch it? Everything changed when **he went into the sanctuary of God.** His perspective completely altered once he spent time with his God. A change in the environment changed his outlook. Just like jumping in the ocean can bring relief to seasick nausea, drawing near to God redirects our minds and hearts. We need a perspective change—we need to go into the sanctuary of God.

Friends, if you are struggling, frustrated, weary, discouraged, or just unable to make sense of your world, go into the sanctuary of God. Read the rest of the psalm. It's a song of hope and life and joy! It's tempting for us to withdraw when life is hard, to pull away from people, community, and even God. But, let these words encourage your heart and steer you to the fountain of life.

Chapter Nine
A MOTHER'S HEART

*Surely he has borne our griefs and carried our sorrows;
yet we esteemed him stricken, smitten by God, and afflicted.
But he was pierced for our transgressions; he was crushed for
our iniquities; upon him was the chastisement that brought us
peace, and with his wounds we are healed. All we like
sheep have gone astray; we have turned—every one—to his own
way; and the Lord has laid on him the iniquity of us all.*
Isaiah 53:4–6

Scared with concern and anxiety about all the unknown, a young mother shared with her small group about a recent health diagnosis. The room felt heavy. She felt confident in God's care but the reality of her burden loomed large among her sisters. In the not-too-distant past, her family had endured a very difficult health struggle with her toddler. Just as this young mom came up for air, another enormous wave pounded down on her.

Then she spoke something so profound. Despite her painful

struggle, she shared her thankfulness she was the one who was sick and not her daughter. She couldn't bear the thought of watching her baby suffer again. Instantly, all the other mothers in the room wholeheartedly agreed. Without hesitation, they would take the pain and suffering over their children any day of the week.

And as I sat there eavesdropping on these holy moments, I thought, "That's exactly what our God thinks too." At the thought of his beloved children suffering the pain and horror that accompanies the wrath and punishment of sin, our Father sent his Son to suffer in our place. The Triune God took on the pain and suffering caused by *our* sin in order that his children would not have to bear it. We were helpless in our iniquity. And so, the Father authored a plan. The Son accomplished it, and the Holy Spirit applies this gift of salvation to our hearts.

The Author of the Universe made his love known to us by giving us his Son. May the reality of the Father's love and the sacrifice his Son has made for your pardon fill your heart with deep love and joy today.

This is your God!

Chapter Ten
A NEW NAME

*Therefore if anyone is in Christ, he is a new creation.
The old has passed away; behold, the new has come.*
2 Corinthians 5:17

My great Aunt B was everyone's favorite aunt. Fun-loving, carefree, and always smiling, she had a warmth and kindness to her that made everyone want to be near her. So, when my mom first introduced my dad (whose name was Charles) to her Aunt B, she asked  him, "What do you like to be called? What is your nickname? Chuck? Charlie? Chaz?" A bit nervous, my dad replied, I go by Charles." She smirked and said, "Okay—Chuck it is!"

She didn't intend to annoy him or make him uncomfortable but to draw him in. By calling him by a term of endearment, she invited him into a personal, warm, and close relationship.

In Genesis 32, we read about Jacob wrestling with God. Fearfully, Jacob prepares to meet his estranged brother Esau. Jacob, whose name means "deceiver or he cheats," had tricked his older brother Esau out of his birthright (Genesis 25) and had stolen his brother's blessing by deceiving his father Isaac (Genesis 27). Esau had good reason to hate his brother, and Jacob had good reason to fear Esau. The night before they were to meet, Jacob encounters the Living God. The Scriptures tell us that a man (whom Jacob later identifies as God) wrestles with Jacob until the break of day. In the struggle, Jacob demands that he be blessed (v. 26).

The Wrestler responds in verse 27, "What is your name?"

"Jacob," he replies.

Then he said, "Your name shall no longer be called Jacob, but Israel, for you have striven with God and with men, and have prevailed."

God changes Jacob's name. He no longer is identified as the one who cheats but rather as Israel, which means, "He strives with God." His past doesn't define him. In addition to a new name, God gives him a new identity. His new identity is completely connected to his relationship with the Almighty God. Interestingly, prior to this event, Jacob referred to God as the "God of Abraham" or the "God of my father Abraham" (Genesis 31:42). But after this encounter, we see that Jacob erects an altar and calls it El-Elohe-Israel, the God of Israel. God had become Jacob's God. He was no longer just the God of Abraham; now he was the God of Jacob, Israel's God. It becomes personal.

You too have been given a new name and a new identity. Just like Jacob, this identity is completely wrapped up in who God is and his personal relationship with you. You are blessed, chosen, holy, blameless, adopted, forgiven, and glorious (Ephesians 1).

Whatever old name lingers in your head, whatever old identity you struggle to shake, remember that you belong to him. We all have those ghosts in our past that try to haunt us with prior failures and mistakes. Names like loser, failure, forgotten, ugly, useless, unlovable, outdated, and dirty. They want to define us. But remember God declares **THE TRUEST THING ABOUT YOU**. You are a new creation; the old is gone; the new has come!

Chapter Eleven
PERSONAL WORDS

*How sweet are your words to my taste,
sweeter than honey to my mouth!*
Psalm 119:103

Cameo is a video-sharing website that allows you to pay celebrities (actors, comedians, athletes) to record a short, personalized message. The cost varies from one dollar to fifteen hundred. It seems crazy to pay such a great expense  for such a short message. But I can see why people do it, even at great cost. People love to have a world-famous celebrity, someone that many people admire and love, speak **personally** to them, address them by name, and share a special message that **speaks directly to their life situation**.

We have something even better! The God who created the universe, who holds the entire cosmos together, and who sovereignly governs and directs every detail of human history **delights to speak directly and personally to you**. The One who knows your situation and your heart better than anyone else in the world intentionally speaks into your life ***through his Word and by his Spirit!*** We all desperately want to be truly known—and we are. We all desperately want to be deeply loved—and we are. We long to have Someone who truly knows us and deeply loves us, intimately involved in our lives—and he is. That's why I love his Word so much! His Word is living and active and through it, he chooses to speak directly and personally into our hearts. And, what's more—we don't have to pay for it because he already paid the price in full.

So today, if you need to be assured that you are truly known and loved, open his Word.

- If you need wisdom that is beyond your understanding and ability, open his Word.
- If you long to know him better, open his Word.
- If you are struggling with sin, open his Word.
- If you are lonely, open his Word.
- If the brokenness of the world around you is weighing heavy on your heart today, open his Word.
- If it seems like many of the relationships around you are crumbling, open his Word.
- If you just want to hear your heavenly Father whisper personally to you, open his Word.

Your Word is a lamp to my feet and a light to my path.
(Psalm 119:105)

It is the Spirit who gives life; the flesh is no help at all. The words I have spoken to you are spirit and life.
(John 6:63)

For the word of God is living and active, sharper than any two-edged sword, piercing to the division of soul and of spirit, of joints and of marrow, and discerning the thoughts and intentions of the heart.
(Hebrews 4:12)

Chapter Twelve
DIRTY DISHES

For we do not have a high priest who is unable to sympathize with our weaknesses, but one who in every respect has been tempted as we are, yet without sin. Let us then with confidence draw near to the throne of grace, that we may receive mercy and find grace to help in time of need.
Hebrews 4:15–16

Michelle spent decades of her life investing in women. She'd bring them into her home, listen to their stories, wipe their tears, and remind them of God's love and faithfulness. Her home was warm, and her heart was trustworthy. One  day, she let me in on one of her secrets: "Honey, I always leave my sink full of dirty dishes when the young moms come over." She continued, "It puts them at ease and reminds them that I don't have it all together and that I understand. When you're a young mom, it's easy to feel all alone, to feel like a failure, to feel like you can't keep up with life. Hopefully, those dirty dishes remind these precious moms that I understand. I was there. I remember."

Those are powerful words. I understand. I was there. I remember.

Sister, these powerful words have been spoken to you by the Creator of the universe. We have a great high priest who **understands us and sympathizes with us.** He knows what it's like to be us because he became like us. He has been there. He gets it.

The Father could have offered a different plan of salvation. I mean he is God, after all. He could have chosen a way to save us that did not involve the incarnation and death of his precious Son. But he didn't. He chose to send Jesus, his only Son, to take on human flesh, to experience life in a fallen world, to be tempted by sin, to be betrayed by good friends, to be misunderstood by his family, to be abused, to be mistreated, and to be killed.

He chose to experience what it was like to be tired, hungry, lonely, and abandoned. He came. And because he came, he can sympathize with us in our weaknesses. From this place of understanding and compassion, he invites us to come to him, to come to his throne of grace, to ask for help, and to find, in him, what our soul most longs for.

Michelle didn't have to leave the dirty dishes in the sink. She had plenty of time to wash them and put them away. But she didn't. She left them there as a reminder that she understood. She had been there. She knew what it felt like to be in that season of life.

How much more does your Savior know and understand where you are? And his response is—come to me.

Chapter Thirteen
INSEPARABLE

For I am sure that neither death nor life, nor angels nor rulers, nor things present nor things to come, nor powers, nor height nor depth, nor anything else in all creation, will be able to separate us from the love of God in Christ Jesus our Lord.
Romans 8:38–39

Enjoying a hot cup of coffee in the morning is one of my favorite parts of the day. I start to look forward to it the night before. Recently my husband started drinking his coffee black. One morning this week, out of habit, he accidentally put cream in his coffee. Oops. As I stood there looking at his cup, I thought, "There's no way you can get the cream out of that." Once the cream gets in, they are inseparable.

Inseparable. Not only does it describe coffee with cream, but more importantly, our union with Christ. Though the Bible speaks often about a believer's union with Christ, he in us and we in him, it can be a hard concept for us to get our minds around. What does it really mean that we are united to Christ? How does that impact my daily life?

Paul writes, *"There is therefore now no condemnation for those who are **in Christ**"* (Romans 8:1).

Union with Christ means no condemnation. Because we are inextricably connected to Jesus, we will never be condemned for our sins. The penalty for our sins has been paid in full and there is no wrath of God left for us.

Paul continues, *"For the law of the Spirit of life has set you free **in Christ Jesus** from the law of sin and death"* (Romans 8:2).

Union with Christ means freedom. We have been freed from the law of sin and death. Because we are connected to the God-Man, we are no longer slaves to the power of sin. He has broken it forever! And we have been freed from the curse of death.

Paul writes, *"**In him** you also, when you heard the word of truth, the gospel of your salvation, and believed in him, were sealed with the promised Holy Spirit"* (Ephesians 1:13).

Union with Christ means the continual presence of the Holy Spirit in your life. We are forever sealed with the greatest Counselor, Advocate, Teacher, and Friend in the world.

Union with Christ means that we can never be separated from the love of God. Nothing in all the earth has the power to disconnect us from the powerful, never-ending love of our Triune God. Because the Son of God has chosen to forever unite himself to you, you are eternally secure in the love of our Father. Today, let your heart feast on this good news.

Chapter Fourteen
GO-TO STORIES

*Oh give thanks to the L*ORD*; call upon his name;
make known his deeds among the peoples! Sing to
him, sing praises to him; tell of all his wondrous works!*
Psalm 105:1–2

When I was a little girl, we had the best dog—Cornflakes. In the mornings, when my mom wanted to be sure that my brother and I were awake and getting ready for school, she would say to him, "Go, get 'em up." Cornflakes would gallop up the stairs, nudge open my bedroom door with his wet nose, and then start to lick my face if I was still in bed. I loved that amazing dog.

Apparently, I tell this story a lot in my home. My kids tease me because as soon as I start with, "Well, you know, when I was in school and getting up in the morning," they quickly interrupt and say, "Yeah, Mom, we know. Cornflakes used to blah blah blah. You tell this story all the time." Unbeknownst to me, it has become one of my "go-to stories."

Most of us have our "go-to stories," the ones we find ourselves talking about repeatedly. Telling and retelling the same stories is something that God encourages us to do! Repeatedly in the Scriptures, the Lord instructs his people to remember his faithfulness and to talk about it continually.

When the Lord sent the plague of locusts to Egypt, he says to Moses:

*Go in to Pharaoh, for I have hardened his heart and the heart of his servants, that I may show these signs of mine among them, and **that you may tell** in the hearing of your son and grandson how I have dealt harshly with the Egyptians and what signs I have done among them, that you may know that I am the LORD.* (Exodus 10:1–2)

When Moses gives God's Law again to the people in Deuteronomy 6, he reminds the people:

When your son asks you in time to come, "What is the meaning of the testimonies and the statutes and the rules that the Lord our God has commanded you?" then you shall say to your son, "We were Pharaoh's slaves in Egypt. And the Lord brought us out of Egypt with a mighty hand. And the Lord showed signs and wonders, great and grievous, against Egypt and against Pharaoh and all his household, before our eyes. And he brought us out from there, that he might bring us in and give us the land that he swore to give to our fathers." (Deuteronomy 6:20–23)

Years later, after Joshua led the people of Israel across the Jordan and set up a pillar of twelve stones from the middle of the river, he says:

*When your children ask in time to come, "What do those stones mean to you?" then **you shall tell them** that the waters of the Jordan were cut off before the ark of the covenant of the Lord. When it passed over the Jordan, the waters of the Jordan were cut off. So*

these stones shall be to the people of Israel a memorial forever."
(Joshua 4:6b–7)

Remember and retell. Remember and retell. What are your "go-to stories" of God's faithfulness? What are your stories of God's mercy and grace in your life? Maybe many memories flood your mind immediately—that's awesome! Maybe today is a day to take some time to look back over your life and remember. Remember the moments when God has been present and close. Remember those times when God wrapped you in a blanket of unexplainable peace. Remember those times when God flooded your heart with love for him. Remember those times when God did the impossible.

Remember and retell. In our remembering and retelling, God strengthens our faith and the faith of our community. Your heart needs you to remember and retell. Your community needs you to remember and retell. What are your "go-to stories?"

Chapter Fifteen
FIERCE PROTECTOR

It is the LORD who goes before you. He will be with you; he will not leave you or forsake you. Do not fear or be dismayed.
Deuteronomy 31:8

Cinnamon is our coffee-colored cow with the thin white patch down her face. Though she looks sweet, don't be fooled. This beautiful, healthy bovine wonderfully loves her babies, and she could not be more stubborn. To say that Cinnamon is difficult to work with is a gross understatement.

This week my husband and I had to gather the cows into the corral, and this girl did not make it easy. On top of the fact that Angus beef cattle do not like to be handled, and are rather strong-willed, Cinnamon is particularly jumpy and skittish. Of all the cows we own, she keeps her distance the most. Often it takes almost an hour of chasing her around the pasture to wear her out to get her to go where she needs to go. It can be exhausting, frustrating, and sometimes terrifying. When agitated, this 1,500-pound animal gets unpredictable and intimidating.

Cinnamon has a calf at the moment. Therefore, corralling this momma now has the added challenge of a mother's instincts. She absolutely will not be separated from that baby. No matter what we do, if that calf does not go into the corral, you can bet that Cinnamon won't go in either. You wouldn't believe the way she can outmaneuver us to guard and protect her baby. Incredibly frustrating, but also rather remarkable and beautiful. She will not leave her baby.

Jesus often used the natural world to explain spiritual truths. Employing parables about creation, he conveys the deep realities of the Father. As I watch these animals on our farm—as their protective instincts heighten, as their refusal to be separated from their babies strengthens—I can't help but be reminded of the uncompromising love of God towards us in Christ. As imperfect and crude as they are, if these cows can be such fierce protectors of their young and absolutely refuse to be disconnected from their babies, how much more your perfect Father in heaven! Creation is but a shadowy picture of the deep, **powerful, unchangeable, and relentless love of God** for those who are in Christ!

As you go about your day, pause and take note of what God has created all around you. Let the simple marvels of creation remind you of your marvelous Creator. If you pass a field of animals and their young, let nature remind you of the One who is on your side, who fights to protect you, and who absolutely refuses to leave you or forsake you.

For he has said, "I will never leave you or forsake you." So we can confidently say, 'The Lord is my helper; I will not fear; what can man do to me?" (Hebrews 13:5b–6)

Chapter Sixteen
AMBASSADORS

Therefore, if anyone is in Christ, he is a new creation. The old has passed away; behold, the new has come. All this is from God, who through Christ reconciled us to himself and gave us the ministry of reconciliation; that is, in Christ God was reconciling the world to himself, not counting their trespasses against them, and entrusting to us the message of reconciliation. ***Therefore, we are ambassadors for Christ, God making his appeal through us.*** *We implore you on behalf of Christ, be reconciled to God.*
2 Corinthians 5:17–20

One morning, while waiting in line for coffee, one of my co-workers noticed a bottle of water in the refrigerated section next to the cash register. She said, "Whoever designed that water bottle is an advertising genius. All I can think about now that I've seen that bottle is—I want to drink that water!"

When she said that, the Spirit immediately brought to my mind this verse from 2 Corinthians 5:20, " *We are ambassadors of Christ, God making his appeal through us."*

We are God's advertisement of himself to the world. In his providence and kindness, he has chosen to reveal himself to the world through us!

We are like that well-designed, enticing, mouthwatering bottle of ice water that invites the world to come and have a drink from the Living Water. Wow! What an awesome and (at times) overwhelming privilege!

But, if you are anything like me you might be thinking, "I am not always a great advertisement for the Lord." Maybe when you read this, you don't feel like a good ambassador at all. You know that sometimes your actions don't reflect the kindness and forgiveness of your Savior. If you feel that way, welcome to the club. You are not alone. But hear Paul's encouragement:

> *Therefore, if anyone is in Christ, he is a new creation. The old has passed away; behold, the new has come.* ***All this is from God****, who through Christ reconciled us to himself and gave us the ministry of reconciliation.* (2 Corinthians 5:17–18)

ALL THIS IS FROM GOD! God has already done the work of making us new. He has already begun the good work of regenerating us, saving us, and making us like him.

ALL THIS IS FROM GOD! He commits to making his appeal to the world through us. What comfort our hearts have knowing that this is God's idea and his Spirit will accomplish this work in us!

If ALL THIS IS FROM GOD, does that make us passive ambassadors? Can we sit back and do nothing? Will God just do his thing while we do our thing? I wonder if Paul thought we might ask those questions. In the book of Colossians, he writes: *"For this [his ministry to the Gentiles—his ambassadorship] I toil struggling with all his energy that he powerfully works within me"* (Colossians 1:29).

Sister, it is true that ALL THIS IS FROM GOD. It is true that God works in you, making his appeal to the world through you. His energy exists within you. **SO GO** and be his light to the world: *"Let your light shine before others, so that they may see your good works and give glory to your Father who is in heaven"* (Matthew 5:16).

Toil with all the energy he is working in you! Reflect his kindness and patience. Be a vehicle of reconciliation and forgiveness in your workplace, in your family, among your friends, in your neighborhood, and in your church. Go and be his ambassador today! Be the beautiful bottle that invites others to drink from the Living Water.

Friend, where does God call you to be his ambassador? Where does he lead you to be a light in a dark place? Where does he ask you to lay down your life and die to yourself? Where does he prompt you to forgive or breathe hope or offer compassion?

He is working his energy in you, sister. Go and be his ambassador as he makes his appeal to the world through you!

Chapter Seventeen
LOOKING BACK

I will remember the deeds of the LORD;
yes, I will remember your wonders of old.
I will ponder all your work, and
meditate on your mighty deeds.
Psalm 77:11–12

This week I talked to a friend facing one major crisis after another at her workplace—major life-threatening illnesses in her family, difficult relationship dynamics, and the grief of losing a fellow staff member. She has been through the wringer.

When I asked her how she was holding up in the face of such difficult days, she responded, "The holding up part is hard and feels dark, but it's easier when I look back and see the trials that the Lord has already brought us though."

Powerful words, and ones that come straight from the Scriptures. Throughout the Bible, God exhorts us to remember. Remember his faithfulness. Remember his promises. Remember who he is. Remember what he has done.

Psalm 74 is a lament over a disaster that has befallen God's people. The psalmist cries out in anguish:

O God, why do you cast us off forever? (v. 1)

Your foes have roared in the midst of your meeting place. (v. 4)

They set your sanctuary on fire. (v. 7)

How long, O God, is the foe to scoff?
Is the enemy to revile your name forever?
Why do you hold back your hand,
your right hand? (vv. 10–11a)

The psalmist is discouraged, frustrated, and despairing. Life seems hopeless. You can feel the desperation in his voice. His cries are honest and unfiltered. How long, God?

Sister, have you been here? Are you there right now? Have you thought to yourself, "How long, God?" or "Where are you, God?"

If you are there, you are not alone. Pour out your heart to the Lord. He can handle it; in fact, he invites us to cry out to him, yell at him, and wrestle with him. Get it all out.

But don't stop there. The entire psalm shifts in verse twelve.

In this verse, the psalmist begins to remember. In the middle of his crisis, he pauses to remember, and he retells himself who God is and what he has done. He recalls God's power and his faithfulness. He remembers:

Yet God my King is from of old, working salvation in the midst of the earth. You divided the sea by your might; you broke the heads of the sea monsters on the waters. You crushed the heads of Leviathan;

you gave him as food for the creatures of the wilderness. You split open springs and brooks; you dried up ever-flowing streams. Yours is the day, yours also the night; you have established the heavenly lights and the sun. You have fixed the boundaries of the earth; you have made summer and winter. (vv. 12–17)

Sisters, remember your God. May the past faithfulness of the Lord serve to encourage your heart today. Remember your God. Preach God's faithfulness to your heart today, Friend. And like my friend, let who he is and what he has done serve to encourage your soul today.

Chapter Eighteen
HE MAKES ALL THINGS BEAUTIFUL

*He has made everything beautiful in its time.
Also, he has put eternity into man's heart....*
Ecclesiastes 3:11

Last week, I looked out my sunroom window and saw four robins searching for worms. Throughout the winter, I have often seen the red cardinals or the bright blue jays sitting on the bare branches. Bluebirds have even frequented the farm. But this was the first robin sighting of the year.

To me, robins are spring birds, the forerunners of warm air, green grass, and long days of sunshine. When I saw those birds, I felt hope because winter won't last forever. That afternoon, even though the temperatures were cold, and the sky was grey and sunless, I was reminded that spring is coming: *"For everything there is a season, and a time for every matter under heaven..."* (Ecclesiastes 3:1).

This verse reminds us that there is a time and place for everything. Seasons come and go. Change is constant. The passage of time brings both joy and sorrow, winter and spring, life and death. There is:

> *A time to be born, and a time to die; a time to plant, and a time to pluck up what is planted... a time to weep, and a time to laugh; a time to mourn, and a time to dance, a time to tear, and a time to sow, a time to keep silence, and a time to speak....* (Ecclesiastes 3:2, 4, 7)

But to me, Solomon's poem about life only brings comfort and hope because of verse eleven. The mere fact that seasons come and go doesn't anchor my soul. The fact that with life comes both dancing and mourning doesn't offer much consolation to an aching heart. But verse eleven brings hope. In speaking about God, the wise king says, *"He has made everything beautiful in its time. Also, he has put eternity into man's heart..."* (Ecclesiastes 3:11).

Here is the hope—God makes all things beautiful. And he will make all things beautiful. Every season. Every sorrow. Every tearing. Every silence. He will make all things beautiful.

This gives us hope. There is purpose behind every single detail in your life—every single moment, even if engulfed in pain, will have beauty. He has put eternity in our hearts. We may not see the beauty this side of heaven, but he has put eternity in our hearts. We were made for eternity. And in eternity, all will be made beautiful.

Sister, God resolvedly works to make it all beautiful. Even though what happens isn't always (or often) beautiful, God commits to creating beauty from ashes (Isaiah 61:3). Wherever you are today, be comforted in knowing that he will make all things beautiful in its time.

Chapter Nineteen

HOME

In my father's house are many rooms. If it were not so, would I have told you that I go to prepare a place for you? And if I go there to prepare a place for you, I will come again and will take you to myself, that where I am you may be also.
John 14:2–3

Last fall, my daughter started her freshman year of college. She loves it, and I am incredibly grateful. Seeing her thrive there brings me great joy.

That being said, we often joke about her rather frequent ***misuse*** of a certain word—**HOME.** Sometimes she'll call me when she's in the car, returning to campus from Target, and she'll say she's heading home. Or we'll be chatting as she walks back from her class to the dorm and she'll mention going home before she runs to the dining hall.

It has become a regular joke of ours because I will **ALWAYS** tell her that she is not going home. Her college campus is not her home. Her dorm room is not her home. As much as we all love it, her university is not her home. Her home is in our small town. Her home is with us. Her home will always be her home until she truly creates her own.

Home—it's such a personal word. For some of us, it invokes warm and happy memories. For some of us, thinking of home brings up pain, abuse, or grief. For some of us, it's a messy mixture. Home is a powerful word.

Jesus says:

In my Father's house are many rooms. If it were not so, would I have told you that I go to prepare a place for you? And if I go there to prepare a place for you, I will come again and will take you to myself, that where I am you may be also. (John 14:2–3)

What beautiful words! Jesus prepares a home for us. One full of love and laughter, one full of joy and beauty. A home where there will be no more sorrow, no more pain, no more abuse, no more sickness. Of all the things he could have said on that last night, he wanted us to know he is preparing a home for us. Home matters to him. It's a powerful word.

Wherever you are today and whatever home means to you, be sure of this—you have a wonderful home waiting for you. You're welcomed and wanted. You belong. You are truly known and deeply loved. It's a place where you have a Savior who says, "I am coming back for you and I'm going to take you home."

Home. May we embrace and thrive, right where we are today. May we love the community and purpose God has given us here on earth. BUT we must also know this—this world is not our home. We have a better home coming. May this hope be an anchor for our souls!

Chapter Twenty
UNPARALLELED POWER

> *Yours, O LORD, is the greatness and the power and the glory and the victory and the majesty, for all that is in the heavens and in the earth is yours. Yours is the kingdom, O LORD, and you are exalted as head above all.*
> 1 Chronicles 29:11

This week, a smoky haze from the Canadian wildfires blankets the sky. Visibility is limited, air quality is poor, and outdoor activities are suspended. We wait for the winds to change, the rains to come, and the fires to subside. As I've sat inside these past few days, searching without success for blue in the sky, I am reminded of how strong and powerful the arm of the Lord is. Despite all the amazing technological developments, the marvelous scientific advancements, and the brilliance of the human mind, no person can control nature.

No one can cause the rain to fall.

No one can cause the wind to blow.

No one can stop the waves from crashing on the sand.

No one can prevent a tornado.

Nature operates exclusively outside of any person's command.

And yet, every fact of the natural world is under control. Divine control.

God makes the sun rise and the rain fall (Matthew 5:45).

God feeds the birds and tends to the plants (Matthew 6:26–30).

God holds the life of every creature in his hand (Job 12:7–10).

God trumps the law of gravity by walking on water (Matthew 14:25).

God calms the raging storm by his invincible word (Mark 4:39).

What a great comfort and encouragement this is to us! ***Our God is unparalleled in power.*** Even the parts of your life that feel utterly out of your control are safely under the unwavering authority of God's sovereign power and rule.

So today, when you look up into the hazy sky, remember your omnipotent God. Let the fog that lingers remind you that what we cannot control, God providentially governs. Your relationships, circumstances, health concerns, mental and emotional turmoil, fear, anxiety, and doubt, all of which may seem to be spinning out of control, are guarded under the supremacy of a loving God. Let your heart rest in the unparalleled power of your faithful Father.

Chapter Twenty-One
TRUST GOD

*For the Lord is good; his steadfast love endures forever,
and his faithfulness to all generations.*
Psalm 100:5

When I am afraid, I put my trust in you.
Psalm 56:3

"Trust God. Just trust God."

Probably close friends have offered you these words and most likely you have spoken these words to those you love. These are good words. True words.

"Trust God. Just trust God."

But sometimes the circumstances of our lives violently throw us up against a solid wall of pain or fear and they force us to honestly confront the question, "Do I trust God?" Do I really trust Him?

"Trust God. Just trust God."

What does it mean to trust God? Does trusting God mean we believe that the circumstances of life will turn out the way we hope? That we go through life oblivious to the realities of brokenness, living in this sort of distant bubble of optimism? That we ignore how we feel and just try to be positive? Does trusting God mean that I believe that he will give me what I ask him for?

"Trust God. Just trust God."

This week I wrestled with this question—really wrestled. And here is where I landed.

Trusting God is believing that God is who he says he is. In every situation and in every circumstance, God is who he says he is.

Trusting God is not banking on what he will *do* but on *who he is*. Trusting God is believing that for whatever life holds, God is always and unchangeably bound to be the same yesterday, today and forever. **He is good.** So when life screams, "This is not good!," our soul answers, "But God is." When fear's voice is deafening, my heart remembers that he is good. When the future seems impossible to handle, he is good. That is our hope. That is our confidence. In him, our trust lies.

Jesus Christ is the same yesterday and today and forever.
(Hebrews 13:8)

Chapter Twenty-Two
GUS

Little children, you are from God and have overcome them [spiritual enemies that oppose Christ], for he who is in you is greater than he who is in the world.
1 John 4:4

My in-laws recently adopted a new puppy. Gus is a teeny tiny seven-pound, fit-in-your-pocket, little Corkie (part Yorkie and part Chihuahua). A few weeks ago, he met my large, 75-pound, five-year-old black lab, Duke. When Gus stands on his hind legs, he is a whopping eleven inches tall. His "ferocious" yap sounds more like a mouse squeak than a dog bark. Duke could easily squash this little guy with one paw.

All that being said, when Gus barks at Duke, my big brave boy quickly dashes into the other room. When Gus stands up on his hind legs, Duke cowers. It's as if he doesn't remember who he is. Duke is bigger and stronger; he doesn't realize he has no reason to fear.

When I watch these two animals interact, Duke's fear seems absurd. Though larger, more powerful, and much faster than Gus, my dog recoils with fright. Surely he could easily overpower this little Corkie in a moment.

Sisters, fear is a powerful emotion. It dominates our thoughts and wreaks havoc on our bodies, causing us to forget what we know to be true. Doubt rises in our hearts—about God, about ourselves, about life. Fear consumes and sends our thoughts into seemingly unbreakable loops of discouragement and despair.

But, God.

Throughout his Word, God reminds us to not be afraid. He exhorts us over and over again by saying, "Do not fear." But, we all know that just someone telling you, "Don't be afraid," doesn't make you not afraid. We need more.

Thankfully, our Father offers us more. He breaks the power of the cycle of fear **with his powerful Word**. Fear does not have the final word over your life! Our heavenly Father reminds us that he is stronger than our fears. And not only that, but he has given us his Holy Spirit, to dwell within us, and his Spirit is stronger than all the enemies of the world. Every evil has been defeated and one day fear's voice will forever be silenced!

Until that day, Sister, be encouraged. You belong to Jesus and you have been given his Spirit. His powerful, undefeatable Spirit. And while your enemies are real and may seem to be unconquerable, You, dear one, need not be afraid. Greater is he that is in you than he that is in the world! So, today, **let your heart and your mind feast on the Word of God.**

Instead of replaying all the what-ifs, let the Better Word of the Gospel be a louder voice than the voice of fear. Remember that your God is with you, he will never leave you, and he is greater than all your fears. He can loosen the grip that fear holds over you. He holds you close. He is at work. You are never alone.

Chapter Twenty-Three
DON'T BE FOOLED

The heart is deceitful above all things, and desperately sick; who can understand it?
Jeremiah 17:9

In August of 2011, Hurricane Irene ravaged her way up the East Coast. She hit land on the first day of our family vacation. Despite the two-day delay, when we finally arrived at the beach, it was breathtaking. The water rippled in a calm rhythm, and beautiful, rare, unbroken shells littered the beach.

Enamored by the magnificent seashells, we spent hours strolling the shoreline, collecting buckets and buckets of unique and colorful gems. We found so many in the sand—undamaged and flawless. That evening, we carefully placed our precious treasures safely in a protected outdoor beach shed.

BUT when we opened the closet the next morning, the

stench was overpowering! The pungent smell of dead sea life attacked our nostrils. It was a cover-your-nose, start gagging, slam the door, and run-away-as-fast-you-can kind of odor! Nothing stinks as much as the smell of dead fish!

Unbeknownst to us, when collecting magical shells on our fairy tale beach, DEAD sea creatures still lingered in their homes. What masqueraded as pristine on the outside gripped only death on the inside.

That is exactly how sin works in our lives. It entices, invites, and attracts. It appears life-giving and satisfying. In the end, it reeks only of death. Sin promises something that it can never deliver. It vows comfort but leaves us with loneliness. It pledges satisfaction but leaves us empty. It offers an escape but leaves us more enslaved than ever.

Friends, we all battle sin. 1 John 1:8 reminds us, *"If we say we have no sin, we deceive ourselves, and the truth is not in us."* And James 1:15 warns us, *"Then desire when it has conceived gives birth to sin, and sin when it is fully grown brings forth death."*

What then is our encouragement as the battle of sin rages within and around us? How do we fight when sin is crouching at our door and seeks to devour us (Genesis 4:7)? How do we stand firm against the lure and temptation of what seems wonderful and satisfying?

Don't fight unarmed. God's Word is a formidable weapon against the ensnaring lure of sin.

> *I have stored up your word in my heart, that I might not sin against you.* (Psalm 119:11)

> *The unfolding of your words gives light; it imparts understanding to the simple.* (Psalm 119:130)

We are all fooled at times by sin—not one of us is immune to its bewitching. But God's Word has the power to defeat sin! The

Scriptures reveal sin's trappings and make us wise against its schemes. Run to his Word. Hide it in your heart. Trust the Lord to defeat sin in you by his invincible word. His Word never fails.

Chapter Twenty-Four
THE JUDGE

*There is therefore now no condemnation
for those who are in Christ Jesus.*
Romans 8:1

I went to traffic court on a citation for which I was undeniably guilty. As the moment in court drew near, my thoughts were absorbed with the judge.

Judges are intimidating; they wield great authority and power. I found myself thinking—what kind of judge will he/she be? Will he be merciful? Will she be angry or in a bad mood? Will he have an agenda of teaching these convicted traffic violators a lesson? Will she scowl? Will he be overly harsh? Will she be out to get me? My fate was in his or her hands. I found myself wishing that I knew someone who knew the judge. Someone who could put in a good word for me.

Judgment and the Judge. The Bible has a lot to say about this. Romans 14:10–12 says:

Why do you pass judgment on your brother? Or you, why do you despise your brother? ***For we will all stand before the judgment seat of God;*** *for it is written, "As I live, says the Lord, every knee shall bow to me, and every tongue shall confess to God." So then each of us will give an account of himself to God.* (Romans 14:10–12)

For we must all appear before the judgment seat of Christ, *so that each one may receive what is due for what he has done in the body, whether good or evil.* (2 Corinthians 5:10)

While we know, with assurance, that for those of us who belong to Jesus, ***"There is therefore now no condemnation for those who are in Christ Jesus,"*** (Romans 8:1), STILL every person will one day stand before the Judge of the earth. The Bible is clear about that. So naturally, the questions surface. What is our Judge like? Is he merciful? Is he angry or in a bad mood? Will he have an agenda of teaching those rebellious kids of his a lesson? Will he be overly harsh? Will he be out to get us? Do we know anyone who could put in a good word for us?

Thankfully, the Scriptures give us some clear answers to these questions! Here is what we know about our Judge:

*Say among the nations, "The LORD reigns! Yes, the world is established; it shall never be moved; he will judge the peoples **with equity.**"* (Psalm 96:10)

*Shall not the judge of the earth **do what is just?*** (Genesis 18:25b)

*The LORD is **gracious and merciful, slow to anger and abounding in steadfast love**. The LORD is **good to all**, and **his mercy is over all** that he has made.* (Psalm 145:8–9)

And what's more, we do know **Someone** who has not only put in a good word for us but has guaranteed the favor of the Judge for us! We read, *"For our sake, he made him to be sin who knew no sin, so that in him, we might become the righteousness of God"* (2 Corinthians 5:21).

And:

But God, being rich in mercy, because of the great love with which he loved us, even when we were dead in our trespasses, made us alive together with Christ—by grace you have been saved - and raised us up with him and seated us with him in the heavenly places in Christ Jesus, so that in the coming ages he might show the immeasurable riches of his grace in kindness toward us in Christ Jesus. (Ephesians 2:4–7)

For those of us who love Jesus, it really is all about who we know. We do know Someone who can put in a good word for us and does (He is always interceding for the saints, cf. Romans 8:34). But what's more is that we know Someone who has given his perfect life in exchange for our sin so that we might rest in the favor of the Perfect Judge.

God has no wrath left for us because he has poured it all out on his Son (2 Corinthians 5:21) in our place. This is your Judge, the One who gave his One and Only Son so that you could be his. When thoughts of condemnation creep into your mind or when the weight of your sin overwhelms you, remember that you know Someone who died to free you from that guilt! You belong to One who adores you and frees you to live without fear.

Chapter Twenty-Five
WHERE ARE THE WEAPONS?

Finally, be strong in the Lord and in the strength of his might.
Ephesians 6:10

Judges 7 narrates the account of when Gideon defeats Midian, an oppressive enemy of God's people. After the Lord instructs Israel's judge on his battle plan, we read:

So Gideon and the hundred men who were with him came to the outskirts of the camp at the beginning of the middle watch, when they had just set the watch. And they blew the trumpets and smashed the jars that were in their hands. Then the three companies blew the trumpets and broke the jars. They held in their left hands the torches, and in their right hands the trumpets to blow. And they cried out, "A sword for the Lord and for Gideon!" (Judges 7:19–20)

Did you notice something odd? The Israelite fighters have

torches in their left hands and trumpets in their right. Where are the weapons? How exactly are they holding swords if they have torches in their left hands and trumpets in their right? Well, they in fact are NOT holding ANY weapons! That's the amazing part. Let's keep reading:

> *Every man stood in his place around the camp, and all the army ran. They cried out and fled. When they blew the 300 trumpets, the Lord set every man's sword against his comrade and against all the army. And the army fled as far as Beth-shittah toward Zererah, as far as the border of Abel-meholah, by Tabbath. And the men of Israel were called out from Naphtali and from Asher and from all Manasseh, and they pursued after Midian.* (Judges 7:21–23)

The Israelites defeated Midian. But there is absolutely no doubt about who won the victory for Israel that day. It was a mighty act of God alone. He gets all the credit and all the glory for the amazing and miraculous victory. Because of his great power, the people of Israel reap the benefit of salvation. And that is exactly the point.

It is all God.

Are you in the middle of a fierce battle? Are you depleted of strength? Have you been trying on your own to win an impossible war? Do you need the Lord to fight for you? Good news! Your God is a mighty warrior. He battles for you—and he will not lose. Like Israel, we reap the benefits of his strength and his grace. The victory over sin is ours to enjoy because our God has done it all.

Chapter Twenty-Six
COLLECTED TEARS

*You keep track of all my sorrows.
You have collected all my tears in your bottle.
You have recorded each one in your book.*
Psalm 56:8

On a ministry leader video call, a sweet woman, through tears, shared about an event she was currently planning. In the midst of coordinating numerous details and laboring for countless hours, she received a criticizing email with wounding negative remarks.

Understandably, she felt really defeated and discouraged. The harsh comments aimed at her efforts cut her pretty deeply. We can probably all relate to that, the sting of discouraging words. Solomon hit the nail on the head—death and life are in the power of the tongue (Proverbs 18:21).

As she expressed her frustration, my heart went out to her. As the meeting progressed, I occasionally glanced at her when a tear ran down her cheek. I don't even know her, and I felt her pain. I don't even know her, and I longed to somehow ease her hurt. HOW MUCH MORE is the Father touched when his children are hurting!

The Father sees every sorrow, every tear, every ounce of pain, and he keeps track of it.

- When harsh words bruise you, he keeps track.
- When careless comments rob your sleep, he keeps track.
- When the sting of painful remarks replay over and over again in your head, he keeps track.

Sister, the Father sees you. He knows. And most of all, he cares. Nothing escapes his notice and *your tears are precious to him.* He keeps track of all your sorrows. He collects all your tears in a bottle. He records each one in his book. You are not forgotten.

Chapter Twenty-Seven
BUILDING HISTORY

In all this you greatly rejoice, though now for a little while you may have had to suffer grief in all kinds of trials. These have come so that your faith—of greater worth than gold, which perishes even though refined by fire—may be proved genuine and may result in praise, glory and honor when Jesus Christ is revealed.
1 Peter 1:6–7

On a dark and foggy night, my daughter and I drove to the beach. Rain was pouring down in buckets, and standing water saturated the roads, terrible conditions for a three-hour car ride. As I was driving, despite the stressfulness of the constant threat of hydroplaning, this thought occurred to me: "I am so grateful for my 30+ years of driving experience."

Because I have driven in conditions like this many times before, I knew that high beams don't work well in the fog.

Furthermore, I could anticipate which parts of the road were more likely to collect pools of standing water.

Experience taught me how to navigate driving next to eighteen-wheelers dumping water on my already overworking high-speed windshield wipers. Even though I never enjoy being behind the wheel in torrential downpours, I was thankful for all that previous storms taught me.

The same is true of our journeys with Christ. None of us wishes for the difficult seasons. We pray earnestly for the stressful times to subside. We can't wait for the trial to be over. We cry out in desperation for relief from the pain. ***And yet, in these tests and trials, we build history with God.*** We experience his faithfulness when we feel abandoned by friends. His Spirit infuses our hearts with hope when despair is our closest companion. He proves himself to be good and strong and present when the circumstances of life threaten to overwhelm and destroy us. We build history with him and that experience serves us well.

So, today if you are in the middle of a dark season, remember: you are building something beautiful with God. You are building history with him. Trust Him. Lean into him. You are not suffering in vain. You are building something beautiful.

> *…now for a little while you may have had to suffer grief in all kinds of trials. These have come so that your faith—of greater worth than gold, which perishes even though refined by fire—may be proved genuine and may result in praise, glory and honor when Jesus Christ is revealed.* (1 Peter 1:3–9)

These verses remind us that we are building history with God. Our faith is being refined and proved. And here's the really cool part: our faith is not tested and proved genuine for God's benefit. He already knows all things. It is for our sake! He tests our faith so that we might know that we know that we know that he is good and that he is real. So, build history with him, Sisters! He will be glorified in it!

Chapter Twenty-Eight
HIDDEN

Whoever dwells in the shelter of the Most High, will rest in the shadow of the Almighty. I will say of the Lord, "He is my refuge and my fortress, my God, in whom I trust." Surely he will save you from the fowler's snare and from the deadly pestilence. He will cover you with his feathers, and under his wings you will find refuge; his faithfulness will be your shield and rampart... "Because he loves me," says the Lord, "I will rescue him; I will protect him, for he acknowledges my name. He will call on me, and I will answer him; I will be with him in trouble, I will deliver him and honor him."
Psalm 91:1–4, 14–15

Two weeks ago, two calves were born on our farm. Seeing these wobbly creatures navigate their first steps over the frozen pasture or watching these unsteady babies first learn to nurse never gets old. It is a miracle every time. One can learn a lot about the Father and his care by observing cows.

The first few hours of a little calf's life are critical. Immediately following the birth, questions rise. Will they be able to stand on their own? Will they nurse? Are they healthy? Are there predators nearby?

In the first moments of their lives, these babies, who will one day weigh thousands of pounds and overpower you in a second should they choose, are fragile and defenseless. Therefore, sometimes the mama will take her youngling away from the herd and hide it in the tall grass. She protects her baby at its most vulnerable stage by concealing it in a place of safety.

While these animals provide a beautiful picture of care and protection, their attentiveness and shielding pales in comparison to the refuge and safety of the Father. In your weakest and most vulnerable moments, your heavenly Father sees you. He knows what you need most and he faithfully provides. In your weakest and most vulnerable moments, the Father takes you away and hides you under the shelter of his wings. **He fiercely guards you because he delights in you.** In your weakest and most vulnerable moments, your God is a refuge of safety and strength. He always sees, always knows, always protects, and always is at work. He hides you in the shadow of his wings. In him, you are safe.

Are you feeling particularly vulnerable today? Do you feel a bit like a weak prey among predators? Does it seem that at every turn attacks are mounted against you? Sister, you are not alone. You are not unprotected and you are safe in the protection of a loving Father who takes great joy in your dependence on him. Take comfort in knowing his care is perfect and you are not alone.

Chapter Twenty-Nine
CHEERING FOR YOU

What then shall we say to these things? If God is for us, who can be against us? He who did not spare his own Son but gave him up for us all, how will he not also with him graciously give us all things? Who shall bring any charge against God's elect? It is God who justifies. Who is to condemn? Christ Jesus is the one who died—more than that, who was raised—who is at the right hand of God, who indeed is interceding for us.
Romans 8:31–34

The Coastal Delaware Running Festival route is a unique course in which participants run to a turnaround point, and then return on the same path. Therefore, at various spots along the race, you pass fellow runners.

My daughter and I loved this! Because each athlete wears a bib with their name and race number pinned to the front of their shirt, as we passed oncoming racers, we cheered for them by name. Many of them turned and looked at us with smiling, yet puzzled faces, perhaps wondering, "Do I know them?" It was awesome to see their faces brighten and their paces quicken as the sound of their name was cheered.

So many aspects of the day remind me of the race we run as Christ followers—the endurance needed, the importance of fellow runners, the highs and lows of the course, the mile markers, the internal and external battles of the race, the thrill of the finish. It's no wonder the image of a race is used so often in the Scriptures!

But what struck me most is the inspiration and drive to finish that infuses you ***when someone cheers for you.*** At several places along the route, non-runners set up chairs and sit by the road waiting for competitors to pass. They shout, "You can do it! Keep going! You're almost there! You're killing it!"

It's amazing the spark these cheers ignite! Inspired by strangers' cries, runners are determined to finish the race.

Now imagine this. There is One in Heaven who knows your name. He plots your exact course, and he is your biggest fan. At every point along the race, he is there cheering your name. When you feel like you can't possibly go on, he reminds you that he is right there with you, and he will never leave your side. When the finish line feels too far away, he points you toward the prize and continues to cheer you on. When the aches and pains of the run make you want to quit, he gives you strength. When you fall, he is there to pick you up, bind your wounds and carry you. He knows every ache of your past, every emotion of your present journey, and he secures your future.

He is for you. He is more committed to you finishing the race than you are! He is cheering your name. He is running alongside you. One day, he will see to it that you complete your race. And on that day, he will be there at the finish line waiting to greet you and thrilled at last that you are home. So keep running, Sister. You have the best One cheering you on!

Chapter Thirty
SATISFY US

*For he satisfies the longing soul, and the
hungry soul he fills with good things.*
Psalm 107:9

*Satisfy us in the morning with your steadfast love,
that we may rejoice and be glad all our days.*
Psalm 90:14

This Spring, we created a bird sanctuary at the farm. In a small section of the side yard, several different types of feeders hang with varieties of seeds. Between the pasture and the lawn, particular bird-houses sit on fence posts. In the mornings, my husband and I enjoy watching **our** birds as we savor a cup of coffee.

What absolutely astonishes me is that it actually worked—the birds came! Prior to hanging the feeders and mounting the houses, we rarely saw a goldfinch. Now

there are brightly colored birds everywhere all the time! There are male and female goldfinches, Baltimore orioles, purple finches, blue jays, bluebirds, red-headed woodpeckers, red-bellied woodpeckers, cardinals, catbirds, robins, sparrows... the list goes on.

What amazes me even more than the fact that they actually showed up (like Kevin Costner in *Field of Dreams*) is that these creatures know exactly what they were created for. The goldfinches visit their specific feeder which is filled with their particular treat. The bluebirds have already nested in the box that is distinctly designed for their kind. The sparrows aren't even trying to roost in the bluebird house. That's not what they were created for.

Nature has a magnificent way of revealing spiritual truths. Each bird is **drawn to** and **satisfied by** something uniquely **determined by their Creator**. They know instinctively what they need to flourish.

The same is true for you and for me. God has created us for Himself and our souls will only ever find deep and lasting satisfaction in Him. In our heads, we may know this, but our fickle hearts seek fulfillment elsewhere. We look to a relationship—maybe it's a friend or a child or spouse—to make us feel loved and valued. We rely on our jobs to give us identity and purpose. We seek food or alcohol or sex to numb the pain or escape the hurt. We lean on our service and performance to make us feel worthy or needed.

Sisters, none of those things will ever satisfy the deepest longings of your heart. They weren't designed to do that and they can't.

What's more—you were not designed for them. You were made for him. Like the birds, **you have a unique longing in the depth of your soul that the Creator has determined to satisfy exclusively with himself.** Only in Jesus will you find the rest and joy your soul craves. He alone brings flourishing. So where are you placing your hope for satisfaction today? To what are you looking for satisfaction and fulfillment? Today is a new day. Run to him and let him satisfy you to overflowing.

> "You have made us for yourself, O Lord, and our heart is restless until it rests in you."
> —*St. Augustine of Hippo*

Chapter Thirty-One

SAFE, LOVED, AND NOT ALONE

*He who dwells in the shelter of the Most High
will abide in the shadow of the Almighty.
I will say to the LORD, "My refuge and my
fortress, my God, in whom I trust."*
Psalm 91:1–2

Nightmares are terrifying, aren't they? Waking up in the middle of the night, shaking, drenched in sweat and tears, surrounded by darkness and panic, believing that all your worst fears have come true.

Nightmares are awful. When little ones experience nightmares, we sprint into their rooms, wrap them in our strong safe arms, hold them close as they cry, dry their tears, and remind them of what is true. They are safe; they are loved; they are not alone.

In the brokenness of our world, nightmares aren't always reserved for sleeping hours. In the wake of trauma or in the midst of horrific circumstances or when daily fear haunts us, life feels terrifying. Anxiety offers unwanted companionship.

While the circumstances of our lives may remain unaltered, our Father desires for us to know that **in him** we are safe, loved, and not alone. He hides us in the shelter of his wings; he secures us in the shadow of his might. He is your refuge and your fortress.

Is there an area of your life where you feel unsafe? Are you battling fear or anxiety? Do the terrors of the unknown haunt your thoughts? Maybe you are plagued with worry over your job, your kids, your friendships, or your marriage. In your secret battles, do you feel alone?

If you answered yes to any of these questions, let me assure you that you are not the only one! God knows that we all deal with fear at times. God knows that some seasons of life can be hard or scary or traumatic. Here is the good news—He doesn't ignore this about us or despise our doubt and insecurity in those moments. Instead, he offers us the assurance of his safety. He reminds us that in him, we are safe, we are loved and we are not alone.

God assures us that we are safe. To assure our confidence in his protection and security, the Father uses four different names for himself in these short verses (Most High, Almighty, LORD, God). It's as if he is shouting, REMEMBER WHO I AM! In our moments of fear and doubt, our Father wants us to put our confidence in who he is. There is nothing more powerful, more wise, or more loving than our God. In him, we are safe.

God assures us that we are loved. In His covenant love, the Father has committed himself to always being with us. Look at all the personal pronouns (word nerd alert!) in these verses—*my* refuge, *my* fortress, *my* God. Your relationship with the Lord is deeply personal. He is YOUR God. He knows YOUR struggles, your joys, your hopes, your fears. Let his personal commitment to and affection towards you remind you of how deeply loved you are.

God assures us that we are not alone. We are hidden in his shelter, safe in his shadow. Shadows in the Bible are consistently connected to God's protective presence.

Life in this fallen world is full of brokenness, fear, and sadness. Yet in the midst of it, God promises us that he is enough. Wherever you are today, remember that in him you are safe, loved, and not alone.

Meditate on the truth of these verses today. Instead of replaying the what-ifs of tomorrow, replay the certainty of God's promise today. Remember that he is our fortress and our refuge.

Chapter Thirty-Two

THE HOUSE OF THE LORD

*I was glad when they said to me,
"Let us go to the house of the LORD!"*
Psalm 122:1

*How lovely is your dwelling place, O LORD of hosts!
My soul longs, yes, faints, for the courts of the LORD;
my heart and flesh sing for joy to the living God.*
Psalm 84:1–2

On Sunday morning, I was captivated by a sweet family during the worship service. Three young children rotated between sitting quietly in their own seats and cuddling on mom's or dad's lap. Dad placed his arm around his son while the boy rested his head safely on his father's chest. Mom gently stroked her daughter's long hair. Brother and sister snuggled closely while trying to whisper quietly. They smiled and felt close to each other. For these precious three babes, worshiping in the House of the Lord on a Sunday morning is a happy place to be.

The House of the Lord—a place of peace, safety, and contentment.

I thought about what a beautiful lesson these parents (perhaps intentionally, perhaps unintentionally) were teaching their children. The House of Lord is meant to be a place where the family of God comes together in joy, safety, and rest. A refuge for the weary. A place of belonging for the forgotten. Home for the wandering pilgrim.

Not because we have it all together, but because we don't. Not because we always all get along perfectly, because that is certainly not true. And not because we're just supposed to put on a sweet face at church because hypocrisy surely isn't beautiful.

Rather, the House of the Lord is a place of joy, peace, and safety because of **WHOSE** house it is. We have a God who personally invites each of us to call him Father. The Almighty Creator of the universe says, "When you pray to me, call me Dad."

We have a God who welcomes us into his house. We have a God who forms and reforms our hearts in corporate worship, a God who showers us with joy in worship even when life's circumstances are harsh and cruel. A God who makes enemies friends, a God who restores what sin has stolen. A God who offers us peace, safety and belonging in his Son, Jesus. A God who invites us to call him Father. A God whose house is one of joy, safety and peace.

> *For you did not receive the spirit of slavery to fall back into fear, but you have received the Spirit of adoption as sons, by whom we cry, "Abba! Father!"*
> (Romans 8:15)

Chapter Thirty-Three
TRUST THE FLOATIES

That which we have seen and heard we proclaim also to you, so that you too may have fellowship with us; and indeed our fellowship is with the Father and with his Son Jesus Christ. And we are writing these things so that our joy may be complete.
1 John 1:3–4

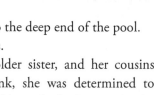

When my niece was first learning to swim, she wore her floaties all the time. These inflatable arm bands kept her afloat whenever she journeyed into the water.

However, even though she wore the swimmies, and they never failed her, she would not venture into the deep end of the pool.

She did not fully trust the floaties.

Even though her parents, her older sister, and her cousins assured her that she would not sink, she was determined to remain near the steps where she could touch the bottom in the shallow water. She felt she wasn't safe in the deep end, and no amount of logical truth convinced her otherwise.

Feelings and truth.

It's challenging to reconcile the two sometimes. What we feel doesn't exactly always line up with what is true. Sometimes this happens to us with prayer. At some point or another, we all struggle with prayer.

We find prayer boring. We become distracted in our thoughts. We question if it really matters that we pray at all. Prayer feels hard. And when we feel this way, we avoid prayer. We're ashamed that our hearts don't feel more joy and excitement about prayer. We feel guilty.

The Scriptures teach us that God calls us to pray, not to exact something from us, but rather that we might receive from Him. ***Prayer is an intimate invitation from the Father to come and enjoy him.*** Even when our hearts are cold or apathetic, the invitation remains. Prayer is the opportunity offered by the Father to experience the pleasure and delight of the fellowship of the Trinity. Prayer is a gift.

Sisters, our hearts (and feelings) often condemn us and convince us that we can't trust our Father. We believe the lie that he really doesn't want ME to come to him. We may think, "He knows how I feel about prayer, and I'm ashamed of that, so he probably doesn't even want me to pray anyway."

Like my niece, we believe the lies that run through our heads instead of the truth of God's Word. I want to remind us of what is true: you are welcomed and invited into the love of your Father. He calls you to prayer in order that you might enjoy him and the fellowship of his Son. You can trust him. When your heart and your mind attempt to convince you that prayer isn't for you, believe your Father. Trust the floaties.

Chapter Thirty-Four
EXPOSING SIN

*Take no part in the unfruitful works of
darkness, but instead expose them.*
Ephesians 5:11

We have an enormous and impressive tree in our front yard. During the spring and summer months, we enjoy picnics, picking crabs, and even napping under the shade of that maple.

Over the winter, it is completely bare and devoid of color and leaf. It appears dead and barren. During the cold season this year, in its nakedness, a huge hornet's nest was exposed. When the tree was full of leaves, the hive remained hidden. But its nakedness revealed that a colony of stinging insects has constructed their home in my tree. Thankfully, because the nest was exposed, we exterminated the hornets, and the potential danger caused by these large wasps was eradicated.

Seeing that hive reminds me of how often we don't know what lies hidden in our hearts. We conceal our sinful parts because it feels safer. Unconfessed sin remains unexposed.

What is more, in our hiding, our hearts deceive us (Jer. 17:9), and sin continues to thrive. Hiding and secrecy are fertile ground for growth. Sin gains strength and power in isolation and darkness. Like the hornet's nest, it breeds buried under cover.

But God loves us too much to let hidden sin continue to destroy us, and he exposes the poison. In his mercy, the Holy Spirit convicts our hearts and reveals what truly lies beneath the surface. And though it's an act of kindness, we don't like it. It's uncomfortable. It's painful. It's embarrassing.

Revealing sin is not a pleasant experience for any of us. And yet, unless sin is exposed, it cannot be removed. Unless confessed and removed, it steals life and causes damage. Just like that hornet's nest.

The Father loves his children way too much to sit by while the Enemy ravages our flourishing. When we confess our sins, God is always faithful to forgive us, to cleanse us (1 John 1:9), and to birth abundant life (John 10:10) and fruit in our lives (John 15:2). Exposing our sins is for our good! Either we will master sin by God's Spirit and grace or it will master us. As God's kindness leads you to repentance today, instead of resisting, trust that life and flourishing are on the other side of this exposure.

Sin is crouching at your door. Its desire is for you, but you must rule over it.
(Genesis 4:7b)

Chapter Thirty-Five
FIGHTING FEAR

*Then Jehoshaphat was afraid and set his face to seek
the LORD, and proclaimed a fast throughout all Judah.
And Judah assembled to seek help from the LORD;
from all the cities of Judah they came to seek the LORD.*
2 Chronicles 20:3–4

Jehoshaphat was the king of Judah when the Moabites, Ammonites, and Meunites came against the people of God for battle. Unlike many of his predecessors, Jehoshaphat did what was right in the eyes of the Lord. So, when a  messenger delivered the news that an enemy was on the way, the king immediately called his people together to pray and to fast. Though he was the powerful ruler of the land, he acknowledged his fear and reached out for help, both to the Lord and his community.

The Bible frequently speaks of saints who were afraid. Abraham feared the Egyptians so he lied about his wife. Jacob feared Esau so he tried to buy him off with gifts. Gideon feared the Midianites so he hid in the winepress. Peter feared the Jews so he lied about knowing Jesus.

Those who belong to Jesus are not exempt from feeling fear. It is a normal part of life in a fallen world.

While the Scriptures exhort us, *"Do not be afraid,"* the Gospel frees us to admit our fears, insecurities, and weakness because Jesus meets us right where we are. The cross proves that the Father's love is secured by the finished work of his Son on our behalf. His promise is not pinned to our bravery.

How then do we respond when fear attacks our hearts? We're tempted to withdraw and hide. But Jehoshaphat helps us. When he was afraid, he sought the Lord, and he asked for help from his friends. He sought the Lord, and he asked for help. **He fought fear by admitting it and refusing to battle alone.**

When we are afraid, God invites us to come and confess our fear to him. Sometimes, he comforts us with his Word. Sometimes, he wraps us in a blanket with the peace that passes all understanding.

But the Lord often ministers his grace to our hearts through the fellowship of his people. When we cry to the Lord in our fear, pain, or anger, he frequently uses the presence of his people to comfort and assure our hearts.

God's people are a tangible reality of his Presence. Jehoshaphat sought the Lord, and he also ran to God's people. The Father pours his love, faith, and hope into his children through the words, hugs, and the presence of brothers and sisters. We are a gift to one another and a means of God's marvelous grace to each other!

Are you connected to the Body of Christ? Is God pouring his faith, hope, and love into you through your brothers and sisters? Are you a vessel of his goodness to those around you?

We have an extraordinary gift in the community God has given us. Wherever you are today and whatever your need, set your face to seek the Lord and run to his people.

Chapter Thirty-Six
CHARACTER IS EVERYTHING

> *So when God desired to show more convincingly to the heirs of the promise the unchangeable character of his purpose, he guaranteed it with an oath, so that by two unchangeable things in which it is impossible for God to lie, we who have fled for refuge might have strong encouragement to hold fast to the hope set before us.*
> *We have this as a sure and steadfast anchor of the soul....*
> Hebrews 6:17–19a

One of my favorite scenes from C.S. Lewis' *The Lion, the Witch and the Wardrobe* comes after a life-changing game of hide and seek. While playing, Lucy and Edmund (the younger brother and sister) enter an enchanted wardrobe that magically transports them into the extraordinary land of Narnia.

This marvelous world fascinates and mesmerizes them both. Upon their return to "real life," with joy and elation, Lucy reports to Peter and Susan (the older brother and sister) the wonders of this fantastical place. On the other hand, Edmund lies and denies the experience.

Although frustrated and confused by Edmund's betrayal, Lucy continues to rave about Narnia. Peter and Susan become increasingly annoyed and angry at their younger sister's insistence on the reality of this unimaginable land. They don't believe her. They even begin to wonder if she is crazy.

Unsure about what to do with her, the elder siblings seek the wisdom of the professor. Expecting him to sympathize with them and offer a solution for their lying sister, the professor surprises them. Instead of agreeing that she is mad, he questions them about her character. He asks them if Lucy is historically a liar. He inquires as to which of the two siblings, Edmund or Lucy, historically, would be more inclined to not tell the truth. In order to give Peter and Susan the answer to their question, the professor appeals to Lucy's character.

Character is everything. As Christ-followers, we bank the entirety of our faith on character—God's character, the foundation upon which all of life is based. **God's character is an anchor for our souls**.

In the Scriptures, God reveals to us who he is so that we might truly know him. Christianity isn't some pie-in-the-sky, ignore-the-harsh-realities-of-life, put-on-a-smile-and-fake-it, way of life. As we face the hurt, pain, and difficulty that accompanies life on earth, God's faithful character is our secure hope.

I'm reminding you today that God is strong, that he is the God of hope, and that he is the God of joy.

Do you find yourself today in a place where you need strength? He is the God of strength.

> *God is our refuge and strength, a very present help in trouble. Therefore we will not fear though the earth gives way, though the mountains be moved into the heart of the sea, though its waters roar and foam, though the mountains tremble at its swelling.* (Psalm 46:1–3)

Do you find yourself today without hope? He is the God of hope.

> *May the God of hope fill you with all joy and peace in believing, so that by the power of the Holy Spirit you may abound in hope.* (Romans 15:13)

Do you find yourself today without joy? He is the God of joy.

> *The Lord your God is in your midst, a mighty one who will save; he will rejoice over you with gladness; he will quiet you by his love; he will exult over you with loud singing.* (Zephaniah 3:17)

Here's the best part: not only is our God full of strength, hope, and joy, but *it is his desire and delight to share himself with you.* He invites you to come to him, to trust him, and to let his character be an anchor for your soul. He may not choose to change your circumstances. He may not choose to restore the broken relationships in your life. He may not choose to heal your body.

But, he will always give you himself, and he is the God of strength, the God of hope, and the God of joy. What an anchor for our hearts!

Chapter Thirty-Seven
MET WITH KINDNESS

*But God, being rich in mercy, because of the great
love with which he loved us, even when we were
dead in our trespasses, made us alive together with Christ
—by grace you have been saved—and raised us up with
him and seated us with him in the heavenly place in
Christ Jesus, so that in the coming ages **he might show
the immeasurable riches of his grace in
kindness toward us in Christ Jesus.***
Ephesians 2:4–7

One afternoon a mother took her son, who has autism, for one of his favorite seaside promenades to watch the boats. However, as much as the young one enjoys the initial walk, he hates to turn around and trudge back.

As they were returning, her son collapsed into his habitual meltdown. As he flailed and cried, people passed by with glares of reproach and dirty looks. Embarrassed, and knowing the outburst could go on for hours, his mom powerlessly watched and waited.

However, on this day a man paused to see if the mom was okay, and she explained her predicament.

Then the visitor surprised them both. Without hesitation, he lay down on the ground next to the boy and gently initiated a conversation. Calmed down by the kind words of his new friend, the three journeyed back to the car. That had never happened before.

The stranger reminds us of Jesus. Like this kind man, Jesus meets us right where we are, even in the midst of our tantrums and outbursts.

Wherever we are on our journey, Jesus is ready to get down on the ground and connect with us right where we are, Time after time, the Bible shows us his compassion and his kindness.

Jesus met Zacchaeus right where he was, up in the tree, in the middle of a crowded parade, with his kindness. He met the man possessed by a legion of demons, right where he was, in the Gentile region of Gerasenes, abandoned by every other human being, with his kindness. He met the woman caught in adultery, right where she was, in her shame and public humiliation, with his kindness.

Wherever you are, that's where Jesus delights to meet you—with his kindness. Are you struggling with depression and anxiety? Jesus meets you with kindness. He is gentle and lowly of heart (Matthew 11:29).

Are you fighting a losing battle with sin? Jesus meets you with kindness. His kindness leads to repentance and life (Romans 2:4).

Are you weary from the heartache of painful relationships and impossible circumstances? Jesus meets you with kindness. He knows what that feels like (Hebrews 4:15). Your Savior is ready to meet you—right where you are. Run to him and rest in his kindness.

Chapter Thirty-Eight
HIDDEN TREASURE

*I have hidden your word in my heart
that I might not sin against you.*
Psalm 119:11

What do these eight items have in common?

- Unwrapped Christmas presents
- Extra money
- Easter eggs
- Wrinkles
- Bad grades
- A diary
- Age
- Secrets

If you guessed things that you hide, you're right! We hide for all kinds of reasons. We stash gifts in anticipation of snooping kids before Christmas morning. We trash report cards because we don't want to get in trouble. We conceal our diaries because they hold private thoughts and secrets. We (try to) cover up our wrinkles because we don't want to lose that youthful look.

While hiding often is associated with secrecy or sin, sometimes hiding is actually the right thing to do. God commands us to hide his Word in our hearts. In the Bible, over and over again God admonishes us to meditate on, savor, study, and remember his Word.

Why? Why is it for our good that we hide God's Word in our hearts?

His Word guides our path (Psalm 119:105).

Do you need direction or wise counsel today? Look to his Word.

His Word makes us holy (John 17:17).

Do you long to grow in holiness and godliness? Look to his Word.

His Spirit recalls what we need from his Word when we need it (John 14:26).

Do you need help remembering God's Word? He has promised the Spirit will help!

His Word brings delight (Psalm 1:1–2).

Are you eager for joy? Look to his Word.

His Word guards us against sin (Psalm 119:5).

Are you fighting temptation and sin? Look to his Word.

His Word is the power of God for salvation (Romans 1:16).

Are you praying for the souls of friends and family you love? Look to his Word.

His Word brings hope (Psalm 130:5).

Do you need hope? Look to his Word.

This list goes on and on. Sister, **today is the perfect day to hide God's Word in your heart**. Whether you're eight or eighty, today is the day. You can do it! His Word is a treasure of abundant blessing. Hide that treasure in your heart.

Chapter Thirty-Nine
PRIDE BEFORE A FALL

*When pride comes, then comes disgrace,
but with the humble is wisdom.*
Proverbs 11:2

At the beginning of my son's freshman year of high school, he and I attended Freshman Student Orientation. As we were leaving the art room, I whispered to him, "I can't believe this, but your teacher has the wrong date for the first day of school on the board."

I even took a picture of the whiteboard because I was so surprised! In my head, the judgmental critic thought, "This is new student orientation! You should probably have the correct date on the board."

Later on, I realized that his art teacher did, in fact, have the CORRECT date on the board. **I was the one who was wrong**! I had the incorrect date in my head, on my iPhone calendar, and written on the large dry-erase board hanging on my kitchen wall.

Oops! At that moment, all that I could think was that I was so thankful that I kept my mouth shut in that orientation!

When I noticed that teacher's board, I was absolutely convinced that I was right. It really never occurred to me that I might be wrong. How arrogant! It was a great reminder for me of the condition of the heart.

I can sometimes be quick to assume I'm right or that I understand the whole story. We all do this. We think of ourselves more highly than we ought. We think that the way we see the world, others, and ourselves is the right way. Thankfully, God reminds us in gentle, and occasionally not-so-gentle ways, that we really don't know it all.

This week, may we ask God to show us the areas where we are blind. Let's ask him to reveal those places where we are so convinced we understand that we don't even consider the possibility that we may not.

Maybe that means taking another look at a fractured relationship or reexamining a present conflict. The Scriptures speak clearly about the pride in our hearts.

Ask the Lord to show you specific areas of pride in your life. Then, repent. May God give us the grace to humble ourselves before him and others that we might grow in grace, humility, and joy

Chapter Forty
SMART CARS

*Look carefully then how you walk,
not as unwise but as wise.*
Ephesians 5:15

I have inadvertently attempted to lock my car while the keys were still inside. On occasion, I even became frustrated at the vehicle in my efforts to lock the door (annoyed that the door won't lock), only to find that my car was protecting me from myself.

Thankfully, my vehicle is smarter than I am. Sensing that the keys remained in the car, the vehicle refused to lock. It safeguarded me against my own foolishness.

Thinking about our own foolishness is uncomfortable. Sometimes our past folly carries the heavy weight of shame and embarrassment with it. However, an honest examination of our own hearts reveals that we sometimes act foolishly. Proverbs 14:12 tells us, *"There is a way that seems right to a man, but its end is the way to death."*

How do we avoid foolishness? What is our "smart vehicle" that protects us from ourselves? Are there means of grace that God has given us to combat folly?

YES! Our God is faithful, and he desires for us to grow in wisdom and avoid foolishness even more than we want to grow! He knows that left to ourselves, foolishness abounds. And foolishness leads to heartache. So, out of his love and grace he provides for us. In addition to sealing us with his Holy Spirit, who is our constant Counselor and Teacher, he graciously gives us powerful weapons against our foolishness—His Living and Active Word and His Covenant People.

Over and over again in the Scriptures, God reminds us that **his Word is a safeguard** for foolishness and sin: *"The law of the Lord is perfect, restoring the soul; the testimony of the Lord is sure, making wise the simple"* (Psalm 19:7).

Every day, we face a myriad of decisions. Some are wise; some are foolish. Should I join that conversation? Should I pursue that relationship? Is it wise to read that book? How do I handle my child's rebellion? Am I compromising in this work situation? Friend, run to God's Word. ***"Your testimonies are my delight; they are my counselors"*** (Psalm 119:24).

Furthermore, the Father has also given us one another as a shield and safeguard against foolishness and sin: *"Whoever walks with the wise becomes wise, but the companion of fools will suffer harm"* (Proverbs 13:20).

We need one another. Brothers and sisters who stand outside of our particular situation are often able to see what we cannot see. This is a gift.

Sisters, the Bible tells us that we all struggle with sin; we all are prone to foolish wandering. But in his love and care, God has graced us with means to protect us from our own folly. Are you reading his Word? Are you surrounding yourself with wise counsel? Like my smart car that protects me from myself, let God's Word and his people be a safeguard for you. Enjoy the rich blessings that he has given you!

Chapter Forty-One

THE EXPERT

*I will remember the deeds of the LORD;
yes, I will remember your wonders of old. I will ponder
all your work, and meditate on your mighty deeds.*
Psalm 77:11–12

Facing some major health issues last year spurred in me a deep thankfulness for my primary care physician. Journeying through pain and uncertainty and knowing that he was right there with me every step of the way brought my heart a tremendous amount of peace and comfort.

And here's why. First of all, **he knows me.** He sees the entire scope of my health, and we have a history together. Recommendations are never offered without considering the big picture. Secondly, **he is an expert** in his field. He is familiar with many different medicines, treatments, symptoms, and how they affect the human body. I can trust his knowledge and wisdom which far exceeds my limited understanding (even with google!). Finally, **the testimonies about who he is** give me confidence. My mother-in-law was an ER nurse for thirty years, and she tells me that when difficult cases would come through the Emergency Department and the doctors on duty needed wisdom, they would call my doctor. His history of excellent and wise treatment, as retold by those who know him well, undergirds my trust in his care.

As much as I love my doctor, and trust in his care for me, he pales in comparison to the love, protection, and provision of our heavenly Father. *The Father knows you* better than anyone in the world, including yourself! From the tiniest detail of your day to the totality of your years, he sees it all. The whole story of your life is under his safe and loving supervision. He sees a picture we cannot yet see. With perfect intentions, he is sovereignly guiding, directing, and governing every aspect of your life for a good purpose. So Sister, put your trust in him.

> *O Lord, you have searched me and known me! You know when I sit down and when I rise up... you discern my thoughts... you search out my path... even before a word is on my tongue, behold, O LORD, you know it... you formed my inward parts, you knitted me together... my frame was not hidden from you, when I was being made in secret, intricately woven....* (Psalm 139)

He is THE expert! There is nothing in all of creation about which our Father is not the leading expert. His wisdom and knowledge are unfathomable, and that gives us confidence. Nothing surprises him or throws him for a loop. Nothing bewilders him or causes him to rethink his plan. Nothing is too complicated for him to unfold. He knows what he is doing; so put your trust in him.

> *Oh, the depth of the riches and wisdom and knowledge of God! How unsearchable are his judgments and how inscrutable his ways. "For who has known the mind of the Lord, or who has been his counselor?" "Or who has given a gift to him that he might be*

repaid?" For from him and through him and to him are all things. To him be glory forever. Amen. (Romans 11:33–36)

Finally, we have **the amazing gift of His Word.** The Bible testifies over and over again to the majesty, love, and power of our God and Savior Jesus Christ!

Sisters, as we remember God's faithfulness throughout redemptive history AND His faithfulness over the course of our own lives, our confidence and hope are secured. Remind yourself daily of what is true. Remind yourself daily of God's personal love for you in Christ and his precious promises to you. He has been faithful, and he will always be faithful, so you can trust him!

Chapter Forty-Two

EVEN DISOBEDIENCE?

> *So they picked up Jonah and hurled him into the sea, and the sea ceased from its raging. Then the men feared the LORD exceedingly, and they offered a sacrifice to the LORD and made vows.*
> Jonah 1:15–16

In the familiar account of Jonah and the whale, the Lord commissions his prophet to go to the great city of Nineveh to pronounce judgment and to call the city to repentance. Jonah, the mouthpiece of the Lord, flat-out refuses. He says no and takes off the other way. Now before we come down too hard on Jonah, let's remember that Nineveh was the capital of  Assyria, one of Israel's greatest enemies. They were an evil and idolatrous nation, deserving the full wrath of God.

So I don't know about you, but I can understand the conflict in Jonah's heart. The story continues—instead of obeying God, our prophet boards a ship heading in the opposite direction, attempting to run away from the presence of his Creator. In response to Jonah's disobedience, God hurls a mighty wind on the sea, and the prophet, along with the other sailors on board the escape vessel, was terrified at the tempest. Jonah 1:5 records, *"Then the mariners were afraid, and each cried out to his god."*

As the storm mounts a greater attack, in desperation, the sailors cast lots to determine who is responsible for the evil that surrounds them. Unsurprisingly, the lot falls to Jonah. To pacify the raging sea, with much trepidation and horror, the pagan sailors throw the prophet overboard. At last, the storm ceases.

While the book may appear to herald only God's wrath and anger, the extravagant mercy and compassion of the Lord are on display. Once the tempest dissolves, the sailors fear the Lord and offer sacrifices and vows to the Creator of the universe. The heathen sailors, who just a few short verses ago were frantically calling out to their gods, now place their hope and trust in the One True God. **God uses the prophet's disobedience to bring glory and honor to his name and to save lost souls.**

Did you catch that? God uses even Jonah's disobedience for a glorious purpose!

What a marvelous reminder of the merciful sovereignty of God in the face of a world full of evil and compromise. Even in the ugly, dark, and sinful acts of mankind, God is in the business of working beauty from filth. While our Creator never authors evil or condones it, he is able to bring honor and glory to himself and blessing to his creation by means of it.

Are you struggling today to reconcile God's goodness with the evil in the world? Do you feel that your disobedience and failure could never be redeemed and used by God for good? These are hard days for sure.

But Sister, be reminded today that God is able to take what is unimaginably wrong and make it right. The story isn't over. Your story isn't over. He delights to give beauty for ashes (Isaiah 61:3).

Chapter Forty-Three
ROAD SIGNS

Your word is a lamp to my feet and a light to my path.
Psalm 119:105

Recently, my youngest child received his learner's permit. While he is driving well and learning fast, I still sometimes have a "death grip on the door" (as he not-so-affectionately calls it), and I pump the brakes on the passenger side floorboard. His inexperience creates tension for both of us.

As he learns (and I fervently pray), I am reminded of how important the road signs are. They are a faithful teacher and guide. They prepare him for what lies ahead (here comes a sharp turn) and alert him to possible danger (steep incline ahead). Expert traffic engineers went before him to prepare the way. The road ahead may be unknown to him, but before he ever navigated these lanes, someone else cleared a safe and navigable path.

In our lives, the road ahead is often unclear. Out of nowhere, life throws us a curve that brings confusion or heartache. We arrive at a crossroad and don't know which way to go. We feel lost, unsure, disheartened. Maybe we struggle with a problem at work, a painful relationship, or an unwanted habit. The next step feels uncertain and difficult. We need wisdom and guidance. Just as expert engineers precede new drivers and carefully place road signs to guide and traffic markers to signal danger, we have an Expert who has gone before us. He too has laid out markers to guide us and alert us to danger.

He has given us his Word.

In our times of uncertainty, he speaks with clarity to our hearts by his Spirit through the pages of Scripture. He knows every journey we wander and accompanies us along every path. And not only has he given us his Word to guide and direct our steps, but God has promised us that he has already prepared each one of our days before any of them come to be (Psalm 139:16). Sisters, immerse yourselves in God's Word. It will not fail you!

As you drive along familiar routes this week, take notice of the road signs. Let them serve as a reminder to you that you have a Father who delights to direct your paths. He has given you his perfect Word as a sure and faithful guide.

Chapter Forty-Four
GOD COMES RUNNING

And he arose and came to his father. But while he was still a long way off, his father saw him and felt compassion, and ran and embraced him and kissed him. And the son said to him, "Father, I have sinned against heaven and before you. I am no longer worthy to be called your son." But the father said to his servants, "Bring quickly the best robe, and put it on him, and put a ring on his hand, and shoes on his feet. And bring the fattened calf and kill it, and let us eat and celebrate. For this my son was dead, and is alive again; he was lost, and is found." And they began to celebrate.
Luke 15:20–24

At the Delaware Seashore State Park, you are allowed to drive your vehicle out onto the beach. You can park your automobile on the sand close to the ocean, set up all your beach and fishing gear, and spend the day by the water. It is especially fabulous for those of us who have a lot of stuff to haul to the beach.

With that privilege come rules to driving on the beach. First of all, driving and parking on the beach are only permitted for those who are actively fishing, and therefore a surf fishing permit tag is required. If you don't own a surf fishing tag, you will be ticketed.

Second, you must have a four-wheel drive vehicle, or else you will get stuck in the sand.

Third, you must have a tow rope, a jack, a shovel, and boards in case you do get stuck.

Fourth, you must air down your tires. In order to be able to successfully drive on the sand, tires need to be deflated.

All of these requirements are posted in multiple places when you enter the Delaware Seashore State Park. Despite the warnings, vehicles always get stuck.

One afternoon while enjoying the beach, an inexperienced couple did just that. The more they attempted to drive, the deeper their tires dug into the sand. This is extremely dangerous because if you continue to bury your car, it may catch on fire. The couple didn't have a fishing tag, the car wasn't four-wheel drive, they had not aired down, and they certainly didn't have a tow rope, jack, shovel or boards. Clearly, they missed the signs.

On one side of us, an experienced fisherman glared at them with disgust and an "it serves them right" kind of attitude. It was certainly true that this couple had screwed up. If they had read the signs, they would not be in trouble. They had created their own mess.

But on the other side of us, a group of men ran to the half-buried car. They got on their hands and knees and examined the damage to the vehicle. They lined up across the hood and pushed with everything they had to get this car back to the hard-packed sand. Working together for quite a while in the hot sun, they helped these careless strangers. It was beautiful.

This couple didn't deserve anyone's help. They had blown it. It was all their fault that they were stuck in the sand. But their foolishness did not keep those kind guys on the beach from sacrificing part of their relaxing afternoon to rush to their aid. They were shown mercy, not because they deserved it, but rather, out of the kindness and compassion of the ones who saved them.

What a good reminder for us—in the mess of our sin and rebellion, our God comes running to our aid. And it has nothing at all to do with our merit; we deserve nothing but punishment for our sin. This is a mess of our own doing.

But God is rich in mercy and abounding in steadfast love and kindness. It is what is **IN HIM** and not what is **IN US** that moves him to save us. He is a faithful Rescuer! So this week when your heart doubts his love, or when you are overcome by your sin, rest in the knowledge that his love for you is unshakable, and he has come to be your Rescuer.

Chapter Forty-Five
GOD'S MASTERPIECE

> *And we know that for those who love God all things work together for good, for those who are called according to his purpose.*
> Romans 8:28

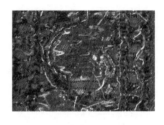

The summer after my junior year of high school, our French class traveled to France and England. While we were there, my mom purchased a small, beautiful tapestry. The detailed stitching is flawless. The timeless art is complete and perfect; it's a masterpiece.

Thirty years later it is still displayed in her kitchen. But if you look at the back side of the tapestry, it's an intertwined mess. The stitching is tangled and matted. No clear pattern or picture emerges. It certainly doesn't look like a master craftsman's work.

Sometimes our lives feel (and even are) like an intertwined broken disaster. Circumstances are confusing and painful. Just as one crisis simmers, the fire of the next is kindled. Chaos and despair seem to trump order and peace. Relationships that ought to be stable and loving bring only heartache and dysfunction. Where is hope in moments like this?

Our hope is found in what the Scriptures teach us about the sovereignty and purposes of God. Your heavenly Father is sovereign over every single facet of your life. There is not one detail of creation over which he is not ruling and reigning. He is Lord of all. Furthermore, **he has unshakably determined that every detail of your life must submit to his good and perfect purpose for you.**

The tapestry of your life may feel like a mess to you. It may truly look or be awful. Sometimes we are only able to observe the underside. Sometimes we are absorbed in the tangled mess. Sometimes the stitching of our lives is ugly and matted.

But, we only see in part. Trust that the Master is crafting.

The masterpiece, though its fullness is yet to be seen, will one day be beautiful because that is what our God has committed to doing for each of his children.

> *He has made everything beautiful in its time.*
> *Also, he has put eternity into man's heart.*
> (Ecclesiastes 3:11)

> *For we are God's masterpiece. He has created us*
> *anew in Christ Jesus, so we can do the good*
> *things he planned for us long ago.*
> (Ephesians 2:10)

Chapter Forty-Six
JUST START

*For it is God who works in you, both to will
and to work for his good pleasure.*
Philippians 2:13

I am one of those people who cries easily at sappy things—sappy cards, sappy commercials, sappy movies, sappy songs—they all get me. I get made fun of a lot for it, especially by my teenage sons.

Recently, I teared up at a commercial for Facebook Portal. The basic story is this: a teenage boy's grandparents give their grandson a set of paints for Christmas. The grandfather paints, and he wants to teach his grandson to paint via the Facebook Portal.

Clearly frustrated, the boy sits at his desk with his sketch pad and paints. He doesn't know how or what to paint. In response to the boy's irritation, the grandfather simply says, "It doesn't matter what—just a line."

In essence, what he is saying is that you just have to start somewhere. It doesn't matter how or where; just start. It doesn't matter if you are confident in all the next steps; just start.

Just start. Sometimes life throws overwhelming obstacles at us, and we feel powerless in knowing where to start in overcoming them. The first step evades us. Ignorance paralyzes us. Maybe there is a broken relationship in your life and though you need to move towards reconciliation, you're clueless about where to start. Maybe there is someone you hope to share the Gospel with, but you don't know where to start. Maybe you're struggling against a sin pattern, and you don't know where to start to break it.

When we don't know how or where to start, the Scriptures remind us that we are not alone. Jesus Christ became a man, and he identifies with us in every way. He understands what it is like to be alone, to be surrounded by broken relationships, to endure painful circumstances, to ask God for a different path (Luke 22:42), to battle sin. He empathizes with us. He knows us.

Furthermore, when he ascended to the Father after his death, he sent his Holy Spirit to be with us forever. To help us. To be with us. To counsel us. To move us towards holiness. To work his might in us. To empower us to just start.

Maybe you sense it is time to take a step of obedience. Maybe you know it's time to begin a conversation of healing.

Remember, you are not alone. Your God is Immanuel. He has given you his Spirit. You don't have to have all the answers because he does. You don't have to know all the steps in order to take the first one. God is with you. You are not alone. He is working in you. Just start.

Chapter Forty-Seven
DOG HAIR

Jesus answered, "The most important is, Hear O Israel: The Lord our God, the Lord is one. And you shall love the Lord your God with all your heart and with all your soul and with all your mind and with all your strength."
Mark 12:29–30

We have two black labs. As you might imagine, when the canines blow out their coats, dog hair covers every square inch of our home. These boys shed profusely. Part of being a Labrador Retriever owner is accepting the fact that black fur gets everywhere. Dog hair clings to my furniture, lives between the pages of my Bible, and even collects in the soles of my shoes  (having walked on the floor with my socks and then put my shoes on). It's everywhere!

As odd as it may seem, being a Christ-Follower is a little bit like being a shedding dog's owner. Just as dog hair invades everything I own and I can't go anywhere in my house without its presence being known, the love of God infuses every area of life.

Before the world began, the Father set his love and affection on a special covenant people. Those of us who place our trust and hope in his Son, forever belong to him. Through the life, death, and resurrection of Jesus, our pardon from the punishment for sin and fellowship with God have been secured. Nothing in all of creation could ever separate us from his perfect, redeeming love.

In response to this never-failing covenant love of God, the Father commands us to love him back with every part of who we are. He wants every single part of who we are. From the deepest desires and longings of our hearts, to the rational logic of our minds, to the entirety of our souls, to everything into which we pour our strength.

He wants it all. ***No facet of our being remains untouched by the reality of God's love for us and our love for him.*** He wants to permeate every detail of our lives. Like the dog hair, his desire is that in every part of our existence, his presence is known.

Where are you today, Sister? Is there a part of your heart that you are withholding from your Father? Are you resisting his call to surrender? Do you offer him parts of who you are and yet keep him at bay with secrets you are unwilling to face? Be encouraged: ***The One who offered his very life for you can be trusted with your love.*** He has proven his love to you by his perfect sacrifice at Calvary. Today, let his presence permeate every single room of the house of your life.

Chapter Forty-Eight
MEANT TO BE SHARED

*Come and hear, all you who fear God, and I
will tell you what he has done for my soul.*
Psalm 66:16

Some of the most attention-getting words are, "Let me tell you a story." When pastors interject testimonies into their sermons, the congregation sits up and listens a little more closely. When teachers share a personal story in the middle of a history lesson, tuned-out students return. Jesus often told stories as he taught. Stories are powerful.

Each of us has a unique story. YOU have a story. Woven throughout your story are chapters of loss and chapters of fullness, chapters of brokenness and chapters of redemption. These stories are meant to be shared. Your story is meant to be shared.

As you open the diary of your life to others, even courageously revealing the most painful pages, and testifying to how God's grace, presence, and healing have transformed your tear-stained heartaches into beautiful testimonies of redemption, the heart of the Father is on full display.

In John 21, Jesus takes a walk on the beach with Peter after his death and resurrection. Only a few days before, Peter repeatedly denied even knowing Jesus. Now they're alone in the aftermath of Peter's failure.

As they strolled, Jesus personally, lovingly, and restoratively ministered to his devastated disciple. In the brief amount of time remaining that the Savior physically walked on earth, he prioritized time with Peter. It was important to Jesus that just the two of them (v. 20) have some time together. He pulled him away from the crowd. He called Peter by name. He affirmed his personal relationship with him (vv. 15, 16). This moment of restoration was absolutely FOR Peter.

But what strikes me is that restoration is **NOT ONLY** for Peter. In these sacred moments, Jesus charged Peter to feed his sheep, to shepherd his people. Peter's healing was meant to extend beyond himself. ***His restoration is a launching pad for future ministry.***

The same is true of us. The marvelous (albeit unfinished) work that God is doing in you is meant to be shared. The story of what the Savior has accomplished for you, and the grace he continues to work in and through you, is meant to be shared.

To whom is God calling you to share the story of his mercy and work in your life? Who might need to be reminded that our amazing God is in the business of restoring broken people? Be assured, there is someone.

Chapter Forty-Nine
DEEPLY MOVED

> *When Jesus saw her weeping, and the Jews who had come with her also weeping, he was deeply moved in his spirit and greatly troubled. And he said, "Where have you laid him?" They said to him, "Lord, come and see." Jesus wept.*
> John 11:33–35

Sadly, school shootings devastate our country. Our hearts ache each time the news comes across our feeds that helpless children and devoted teachers are victimized by the cruelty of gun violence. Words seem inadequate. Tears flow. Questions mount.

How do we make sense of such cruel violence?

How do we reconcile the goodness of God with such horrific attacks?

What comfort do we have in the midst of overwhelming sadness and horror?

In the Gospel of John, we read about the death of a man named Lazarus. Through this account, we get a beautiful glimpse into the heart of God, more specifically, the heart of God in the midst of human sadness and death.

At the beginning of Chapter 11, we read that Lazarus is sick. So Mary and Martha (his sisters) send word to their friend Jesus to come because they know that he loves Lazarus (v. 3). However, by the time Jesus arrives at Bethany, it's too late. Lazarus has been in the tomb for four days (v. 17).

Now Jesus, being the Resurrection and the Life (v. 25), knows that this illness will not end in death (v. 4). He knows that he is going to raise Lazarus from the dead and that he is going to call him out of that tomb (v. 43). Moreover, he also tells his disciples that this entire event is for the glory of God and that he, the Son of God, will be glorified through it (v. 4).

The Author of Life has written this story. And it is a glorious, miraculous, amazing story with a very happy ending!

So why on earth does Jesus get so upset? Why on earth, when he sees the weeping sisters, is he deeply moved and greatly troubled (v. 33)? Why on earth does Jesus weep (v. 35)? In just a few moments, he is going to call the name of that dead man and Lazarus is going to walk out of the tomb (vv. 43–44)! So, why all the emotion? Why is he distraught if he knows how this story will turn out in the end?

Because the heart of our God is moved by human sadness and suffering. It matters to him. A lot. The tears of the sisters who lost their brother, the tears of the Jews who were with them, and his own affection for Lazarus, bring the God-Man himself to tears. He is close to the broken-hearted. He draws near to those who are crushed. He enters into the pain and suffering of those he loves. That is the heart of our God.

When questions remain unanswered, when evil seems to win, when violence abounds, when the goodness of God is clouded by the brokenness of our world—we remember our God. We cling to what we know to be true about the heart of the One who has the whole world in his hands.

Wherever you are today, may your heart find hope and

strength in knowing that Jesus is close. The pain of the world matters to him. He is not unmoved by the suffering of our world even though he will make all things right one day. So, run to him. Run to the One who is deeply moved by your tears. Run to the One who moves towards you in your pain. Run to the One who weeps with those who weep.

Chapter Fifty
AIR FRYERS

And I heard a loud voice from the throne saying, "Behold, the dwelling place of God is with man. He will dwell with them, and they will be his people, and God himself will be with them as their God. He will wipe away every tear from their eyes, and death shall be no more, neither shall there be mourning, nor crying, nor pain anymore, for the former things have passed away."
Revelation 21:3–4

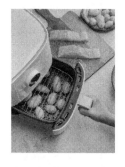

Whenever we get a new appliance or gadget, my husband asks me if I read the instructions manual. At this point, that question is comical to me because I always respond with the same answer—nope! I have no desire nor intention whatsoever of ever reading those instructions. I don't really need to know **HOW** the new air fryer works; I just want it to work.

Sometimes we experience seasons of deep loss and pain. The heaviness of sorrow settles on us like a dark cloud. The reality of the ruins of this broken world sit like an immovably heavy weight on our souls. Sadness overshadows every conversation, every meal, every movement. Death, anxiety, depression, fear. Tears come like uninvited guests at unannounced moments.

You've experienced these seasons.

Thankfully, God frequently addresses sorrow, death, and sadness in the Scriptures. He knows that pain and suffering are unwelcome companions in this life. If you are in the middle of a hard week or a hard decade, hear these words: ***Your hurt does not escape the Father's notice.***

He sees every tear that rolls down your cheek. He hears every muffled cry that you bury in your pillow. He understands every feeling of doubt, fear, despair or anger that invades your soul. Your hurt does not escape his notice.

What's even more amazing—not only does he notice our affliction, he is redeeming it! One day, all the pain and suffering will be gone. One day, all our mourning will be turned into dancing (Psalm 30:11). One day, every wrong will be made right.

We don't have to know ***HOW*** that will happen in order for us to know that it will happen. Even when we can't understand **how** mourning will be turned into joy, we know that it will. Just like that air fryer, we really don't need to understand **how** he will work that all out. We just know he will. What hope we have!

Chapter Fifty-One
EVERYONE IS LOOKING FOR YOU

And rising very early in the morning, while it was still dark, he (Jesus) departed and went out to a desolate place, and there he prayed. And Simon and those who were with him searched for him, and they found him and said to him, "Everyone is looking for you."
Mark 1:35–37

Do you create to-do lists? I sure do. First, I draw a small box on the top line. Next, the task to be accomplished is noted. When completed, the box is checked and the description is crossed out (preferably with a black Sharpie). Double satisfaction! A checkmark in the box and a dark line across the chore.

Often, if I forget to put something on the to-do list, but when I do in fact finish the task, I go back, draw the box, write the completed task on the list, and then check the box and cross it out!

Most of us have a list of goals we expect to achieve each day: work-related tasks, household errands, medical appointments, caring for people, ministry work, and social activities. Our lives are full and busy. We are pulled in a thousand different directions. Sometimes it feels as though we hardly have enough time in the day to get it all done.

Jesus understands that feeling. He was in great demand (even greater demand than you are); everyone was looking for him. He had so much to do. Urgent needs surrounded him. Desperate people clung to him. His mission was paramount.

And he often withdrew.

He woke up early, and he distanced himself from the crowds and the distractions. He left what was urgent so he could meet his greatest need, communion with his Father. All other tasks were subservient to prayer.

Sisters, we too need to be with our Father—alone, undistracted, away from the desperate needs of the moment. Time with God reorients our hearts and minds.

There is always more on the to-do list. There are constantly urgent pressing needs. There are people who regularly require your attention. But if Jesus, whose mission was far more important than yours or mine and who had far more people demanding his time, regularly withdrew to pray, how much more is it vital for our flourishing?

Are you feeling pressed by the tyranny of the urgent? Do you have too much to do and not enough time to do it? Are the demands for your time, energy, and heart overwhelming you today?

The Father invites you to come to him. To sit at his feet. To pray. To refocus. To rest. To be refreshed. Accept the invitation. Make the time. Enjoy the moment.

> "I have so much to do that I shall spend the first three hours in prayer."
> —*Martin Luther*

Chapter Fifty-Two
THE RESCUER

"When we were utterly helpless, Christ came at just the right time and died for us sinners. Now, most people would not be willing to die for an upright person, though someone might perhaps be willing
to die for a person who is especially good. But God showed his great love for us by sending Christ to die for us while we were still sinners."
Romans 5:6–8 (NLT)

During the summer of 2021, on the popular vacation route to Ocean City, Maryland, one humble man became a life-saving hero. Following a multiple-car crash on the Maryland Route 90  bridge, a two-year-old toddler was ejected from a pick-up truck dangling over the side of a guardrail. A Good Samaritan jumped off of the twenty-five-foot bridge into the water and rescued the helpless young child who was floating face down in the water.

The story brought me to tears as I thought about the heart of the rescuer—his bravery, his sacrifice, his strength. He put his own life at risk to save a stranger. He saw a crisis need and immediately responded, even knowing the cost was high.

What if he injured himself when his body impacted the water?

What if he didn't survive the jump?

What if he wasn't strong enough to bring the little girl to safety?

You also have a Rescuer, someone who plunged into the darkness of sin and death to save you, a helpless, face-down struggler, utterly powerless to rescue yourself. Even before you wanted to be rescued. Even when you were the enemy of the Rescuer. Before the foundation of the world was laid, the plan was set in motion for your redemption. The Father knew the depth of your sin and your need for salvation. So he sent his Son to accomplish the mission.

Unlike the highway hero, your Rescuer was injured when he saved you. In fact, he was beaten so badly that he was unrecognizable (Isaiah 52:14).

Unlike the highway hero, your Rescuer didn't survive the jump.

Unlike the highway hero, your Rescuer knew he was strong enough to bring you to safety.

Today—if you hear an emergency vehicle quickly approaching, if you pass a collision littered with ambulances and police cars, if the local evening news reports a fire, let the first responders of your town be a reminder that you too were rescued and at a great, great cost to the One who authored your redemption. Your salvation cost him his precious Son. You are that loved.

Chapter Fifty-Three
CAN'T KEEP IT IN!

*As he was drawing near—already on the way down the
Mount of Olives—the whole multitude of his disciples
began to rejoice and praise God with a loud voice for all
the mighty works that they had seen, saying, "Blessed is the King
who comes in the name of the Lord! Peace in heaven and glory
in the highest!" And some of the Pharisees in the crowd said
to him, "Teacher, rebuke your disciples." He answered, "I tell
you, if these were silent, the very stones would cry out."*
Luke 19:37-40

When my youngest was little, it was nearly impossible for him to keep secret the gifts he purchased for his siblings. He just couldn't hold it in!

Whenever he picked out a birthday gift or a Christmas present, within moments he had to tell the recipient what he bought. It took every ounce of willpower for him to wait until the celebration day.

Even if he could delay the offering, he just had to give clues as to what the gift was. One year, he selected the perfect, super-soft, fleece pajama pants for his sister, and he was thrilled. Upon returning home from the mall, he darted up to his sister's room and explained, "I'm not telling you what I got you, but it starts with 'puh' and rhymes with muh-jamas." Super sneaky.

When Jesus entered Jerusalem on Palm Sunday, the crowds rejoiced and praised God with a loud voice and shouted, *"Blessed is the King who comes in the name of the Lord! Peace in heaven and glory in the highest"* (Luke 19:37–38). The Pharisees were indignant and ordered Jesus to rebuke his disciples. In response to their anger, Jesus answered, *"I tell you, if these were silent, the very stones would cry out"* (Luke 19:40). If the people didn't shout out their praise at the magnitude of God's unfolding drama, the rocks would.

Fast forward just a few days.

Jesus is on the cross. He breathes his last breath. He gives up his spirit. It is the moment of greatest triumph in human history. The price for sin has been paid in full. The wrath of God toward his people has forever been satisfied. Condemnation: eliminated. Atonement for sin: accomplished.

But no one is celebrating.

No one is crying out in praise.

And Jesus cried out again with a loud voice and yielded up his spirit. And behold, the curtain of the temple was torn in two, from top to bottom. ***And the earth shook, and the rocks were split.*** (Matthew 27:51)

The rocks split! The rocks cried out! Just like Jesus foretold! They couldn't keep it in.

Like my little boy, the earth just couldn't contain her joy! Creation SHOUTED as the Son of God triumphed once and for all over sin and death!

Oh God, may we truly celebrate today, and for all our days, the triumph you have guaranteed for us by your death and resurrection!

Chapter Fifty-Four
COMING FOR YOU

*And the Word became flesh and dwelt among us,
and we have seen his glory, glory as of the only Son
from the Father, full of grace and truth.*
John 1:14

There are often piles and piles of dirty clothes at my house, and it's easy for the laundry to stack up. The baskets overflow. The dryer needs to be emptied.

No matter how caught up I may get, it just keeps coming. Even if every piece of clothing in the house is clean at noon (which never happens), by the end of the day there will be more dirty clothes. It is never-ending.

This week at a staff gathering, our pastor shared a short devotion. He talked about the beauty of the incarnation, how Jesus Christ, the Son of God, became a man and **came for us**.

He continued, "Jesus says to us, '**Not only did I come, but I will never stop coming for you. I will never stop coming for you.**'" Those words are simple and profound. Jesus will never stop coming for us. He will never stop coming for you. Those of us who belong to him have been sealed by his spirit. We belong to him forever. ***He never tires of coming to us.***

When we're weak, he comes.
When we're hurting, he comes.
When we're angry, he comes.
When we're apathetic, he comes.
When we're burdened by sin, he comes.
When we're lonely, he comes.
When we're full of joy, he comes.
When we want to hide, he comes.

He never stops coming to us. This is the glory of the incarnation! We celebrate that he has come, that he will one day come again to the earth and ALSO that every day he comes to us, through his Word and by his Spirit.

Again and again. Never tiring. Never stopping.

So this week, when you see that pile of laundry sitting in the basket (or on the bathroom floor), remind yourself that just as the dirty clothes never stop coming, the Incarnated Jesus will never stop coming to you either. He has come, he will come, and he does come to you.

Chapter Fifty-Five
CALLED INTO EXISTENCE

*That is why it **depends on faith**, in order that the promise **may rest on grace** and be guaranteed to all his offspring—not only to the adherent of the law but also to the one who shares the faith of Abraham, who is the father of us all, as it is written, "I have made you the father of many nations"—in the presence of the God in whom he believed, **who gives life to the dead and calls into existence the things that do not exist.** In hope he believed against hope, that he should become the father of many nations, as he had been told, "So shall your offspring be." He did not weaken in faith when he considered his own body, which was as good as dead (since he was about a hundred years old), or when he considered the barrenness of Sarah's womb. No unbelief made him waver concerning the **promise of God**, but he grew strong in his faith as he gave glory to God, **fully convinced that God was able to do what he had promised**.*
Romans 4:16–21

One February, I attended a conference in Atlanta, and it was cold. I looked out of my hotel window and noticed this man

sunbathing beside the pool without his shirt. It was 48° outside! That seems a little cool for anyone to be sitting by the pool catching some rays. From the photo, notice the wardrobe of women who are also sitting in the courtyard. They are wearing sweaters and heavy winter coats!

I have no idea what our pool lounger was thinking, but he reminded me of the verse from Romans 4 that says God calls things into existence that are not. I thought... maybe he is just going to try to call that warm weather into existence. Maybe if he acts as if it is sunny and hot, by some power of positive thinking and believing, he will beckon that sunny weather into existence. It sounds silly, doesn't it?

Even though it certainly does not work that way with weather, the impossible notion of calling something into existence that does not exist **IS** within the realm of possibility for God. In fact, that is exactly how God works!

Abraham believed God despite how his circumstances looked. It would've been easy (and understandable) for Abraham to disbelieve that God could make him the father of many nations. After all, he and Sarah were both old and past the age of childbearing.

Yet, he trusted God. He focused more on the power of Almighty God than he did on himself or his circumstances. The same is true of us. When I look at the "impossibility" of life's circumstances: a family member's coldness of heart, unconsolable loss, deep brokenness within my own heart, the prison of anxiety, the unbeatable war with sin, what seems like "unhealable" wounds—my heart can easily become discouraged. Doubts loom large.

BUT, when my eyes are on him, the One who does the impossible, when I remember who God is, the One who calls things into existence that do not exist, my soul is strengthened. Maybe right now you are in the midst of hopeless situations— painful circumstances, difficult relationships, overwhelming tension, and grief. You can't imagine how God could bring good out of your situation.

Sister, remember who God is. Let your thoughts linger more on who he is than on who you are.

He sees you, he knows you and he is at work. He is strong. He is powerful. He is sovereign. And he is in the business of calling into existence things that do not exist!

Chapter Fifty-Six
LESSONS FROM GOLF

*But as for you, teach what accords with sound doctrine...
Older women likewise are to be reverent in behavior, not
slanderers or slaves to much wine. They are to teach what is good,
and so train the young women to love their husbands and children,
to be self-controlled, pure, working at home, kind, and submissive
to their own husbands, that the word of God may not be reviled.*
Titus 2:1–5

Over the past two years I have been learning (albeit very slowly) how to play golf, which is both enjoyable and frustrating. Recently, while playing (unsuccessfully I might add!) with my son, I thought, "I really need another golf lesson."

You see, it does me absolutely no good to spend hours practicing a chip shot with a flawed technique—bad habits only grow. Without the guidance and knowledge of someone else, someone who successfully chips the ball up onto the green, I am at a true loss. To have my own personal golf pro who walks beside me, coaches me, and helps me learn how to enjoy and play the game well—how advantageous that would be!

Life is a lot like golf. It's good to have someone walk beside you through the ups and downs and the joys and the sorrows of life That's an enormous blessing.

Our Creator hard-wired us to hunger for and be nourished by community—to journey through life together—to encourage, correct, love, and challenge one another.

In Paul's letter to Titus, the author gives specific instructions to men and women on godly living. The apostle instructs the older women to teach the younger women, to walk beside them, to offer guidance, to give instruction, and to correct when necessary.

He offers us ***an incredible blessing in the command*** to mentor and be mentored by one another. Sisters, ***God's commands unfailingly connect to his blessings because they perfectly reflect the Father's heart.*** He knows both the profound joy we experience in community and the deficiency we suffer without it.

No matter your age or stage, instructing the younger and receiving instruction from the older remains your calling. A blessing and a command.

We are each other's golf pros!

So, how about you? Are you in a mentoring relationship, whether formally or informally? Who is God calling you to walk alongside as the "older" woman? Maybe it's a younger colleague at work, a neighbor, or your daughter? Who is intentionally walking alongside you?

Sisters, take advantage of this gift from the Lord!

Chapter Fifty-Seven
MAKE US FAITHFUL

*Now to him who is able to do far more abundantly than
all that we ask or think, according to the power at work
within us, to him be glory in the church and in Christ Jesus
throughout all generations, forever and ever. Amen.*
Ephesians 3:20–21

One Sunday morning during a church service in the United States, a Chinese missionary on sabbatical shared about the suffering and various trials that accompany proclaiming the Gospel in a foreign (often hostile) environment. The American interviewer asked how their local church might pray for missionaries abroad. The evangelist responded, "As Americans, you often pray that God eases your suffering... that he takes away your pain... that he removes your trials."

He continued, "That's not how we pray. We pray that God makes us faithful. We pray that in the middle of the suffering, persecution and very difficult days, that God makes us faithful to him."

The Holy Spirit convicted me with those words. Often my prayers merely ask God for a reprieve from the pain, relief from the suffering, or the removal of great trials. What I long for is the absence of hard things.

However in pondering his words, "We pray that God makes us faithful," my prayer changed. God began the good work of reforming my heart to be like his, to long to be faithful whatever the day may hold.

Listen to this encounter between Jesus and Peter:

Simon, Simon, behold, Satan demanded to have you, that he might sift you like wheat, but I have prayed for you that your faith may not fail. And when you have turned again, strengthen your brothers. (Luke 22:31–32)

Jesus prays that Peter would be faithful. He doesn't ask the Father to remove Peter's suffering. He doesn't pray that every obstacle in Peter's way dissolves. He doesn't ask for Peter's life be free of pain or heartache. No. He prays that Peter would be faithful.

O Father, give me a heart that longs to be faithful to you. When suffering and pain are constant unwanted companions, Spirit, make me a faithful follower of Christ. I need your help. Thank you for interceding for me even now. And for those who are suffering at the hands of evil across the globe, may your Church be faithful... faithful to pray, faithful to love, and faithful to herald the Gospel. We ask for you to have mercy on the people who are cruelly persecuted for their faith. Strengthen their souls. Thank you for your faithfulness to us and to your people. Our hearts cry all the more, "Come, Lord Jesus!"

Chapter Fifty-Eight
PULL THE WEEDS

If you do well, will you not be accepted? And if you do not do well, sin is crouching at the door. Its desire is for you, but you must rule over it.
Genesis 4:7

Each Spring, the hope of new life and fruitful growth abound. Green grass, budding trees, blooming flowers—all signs announcing new beginnings.

But with all the beauty and hope that come with the season, there are also pesky weeds that invade and attempt to destroy the flourishing of creation. Weeds. Weeds. Weeds. They suck the life out of everything that surrounds them. They spread uncontrollably. The longer they go untended, the more stubborn they become. AND, they deceive. As the buds sprout, it's often hard to tell if the green shoot is a weed or a flower.

Before long though, the true identity of the plant is revealed.

Then the work of removal begins. If you extract the weeds

when they're young, and if you uproot the entire weed—pulling at the base and including the root—they are eradicated. But if you wait until the roots are firmly established, it is much tougher to fully do away with these life-killers.

Sin works in much the same way. It seeks to suck the life out of everything it touches. It spreads uncontrollably. The longer it goes untended, the stronger its roots become. It masquerades as life-giving, but really only steals, kills, and destroys.

Therefore, Jesus calls us to deal with our sin in radical ways.

If your right eye causes you to sin, tear it out and throw it away. For it is better that you lose one of your members than that your whole body be thrown into hell. And if your right hand causes you to sin, cut it off and throw it away. For it is better that you lose one of your members than that your whole body go into hell. (Matthew 5:29–30)

Sin is powerful and deadly; its grip enslaves us. We all must battle it (1 John 1:8). No one is immune to its poison. It is not to be taken lightly, overlooked, or ignored. Jesus commands us to get rid of it, to fiercely engage in the war to eradicate it!

While he is not literally saying that we should cut out our eye, he speaks forcefully and authoritatively. Sin should be entirely removed! His words are commanding. It is a matter of life and death!

Sister, where are you today? Are you flirting with sin? Are you deeply entrenched in what feels like an unbreakable hold? Is sin promising you life today?

Don't be fooled. Sin will not deliver what it offers.

So, fight! Fight against the lie that it's not that dangerous. Fight against the lie that it will not enslave you. Fight against the lie that you can handle this on your own. And fight against the lie that you can't overcome it.

You have One who has conquered the power of sin, hell, and

death fighting on your behalf! He has won the victory over sin, and he wars with and for you. So, run. Flee from sin. Confess it. Kill it. And BE FREE!

Chapter Fifty-Nine
JUST A WORD

And the men marveled, saying, "What sort of man is this, that even winds and sea obey him?"
Matthew 8:27

In 2022, Hurricane Ian ravaged Florida. With winds up to 259 mph, this coastal tempest was the fifth-strongest storm to ever strike the United States.

Natural disasters remind us of the untamable power of nature. Regardless of the greatest plannings, tropical tornadoes are uncontrollable. No amount of sand keeps the waves from crashing beyond their borders. Wind gusts defy restraining. Violent storm surges are impossible to slow or stop. Torrential rain and floods effortlessly carve their way along streets and through neighborhoods destroying everything in their way. The magnitude of such force inspires both fear and awe.

In spite of the most valiant efforts, even with the wonders of twenty-first-century technology and notwithstanding the genius of the human mind, in moments like this, we understand again that ***life is out of our control.*** The inability to coerce or manipulate nature demands that humanity come face to face with our limitations, powerlessness, and weakness. In many ways, we are at the mercy of the tempest.

Yet, in the middle of ONE storm, a stark contrast emerges.

And a great windstorm arose, and the waves were breaking into the boat, so the boat was already filling. But he was in the stern, asleep on the cushion. And they woke him and said to him, "Teacher, do you not care that we are perishing?" And he awoke and rebuked the wind and said to the sea, "Peace! Be still!" And the wind ceased, and there was a great calm. (Mark 4:37–39)

With just a word, Jesus overpowers the storm. With just a word, nature obeys his command. With just a word, all is calm.

Just a word.

Sisters, this is your God. For sure, life is out of our control, and it is important for us to be reminded of this truth. For sure, much like a destructive storm, the circumstances and relationships of our days wreak havoc on our lives.

But they are not untamable. Our God is stronger. There is nothing outside of God's sovereign control. He has authority over every single detail of creation. Let the powerfulness of the storm remind you of just how fiercely mighty your God is. **With just his word, he controls and commands the entire universe.** Whatever you are facing today is not outside of his control—no matter how chaotic or powerful your storm seems.

Meditate on this truth today, Sister. Your God is undefeatable; you are in good hands.

Chapter Sixty
BUILDING A GRATEFUL HEART

Give thanks to the LORD, for he is good, for his steadfast love endures forever. Give thanks to the God of gods, for his steadfast love endures forever.
Psalm 136:1–2

The Great Pyramid of Giza in Egypt is one of the seven ancient wonders of the world. This amazing burial ground stands 147 meters tall and for 3800 years remained the tallest man-made structure in the world. The  pyramid stood as witness to the world of beauty, strength, and magnificence.

Construction went on for twenty years, twenty years of back-breaking manual labor, day after day, year after year, decade after decade. Furthermore, the impressive structure required 2.5 million individually cut stone blocks. Each block was erected and positioned one at a time. It was a slow process.

Building a heart of thankfulness is a lot like the Great

Pyramid of Giza. A heart of gratitude speaks to the world of the beauty, goodness, and majesty of God. A grateful heart doesn't happen overnight, but is a slow process. A thankful heart is built one stone at a time.

Psalm 136 begins and ends with a call to give thanks. Sandwiched between that call, the psalmist instructs us about why and how we are to give thanks. In every single verse from 1–26, this refrain repeats, *"for his steadfast love endures forever."*

The steadfast love of God anchors every offering of thanksgiving. **Every act of God in your life is rooted in his forever-enduring steadfast love.** It never changes. It never fails. It never comes up short. So we give thanks because of his unwavering, resolute affection towards us.

Psalm 136 teaches us that God demonstrates his love towards us as he cares for us in the large and small details of our daily lives. ***David cultivates a heart of thankfulness by offering specific thanks for the specific gifts from God one thankful prayer at a time.*** David names particular events individually to remind himself of the goodness and love of God.

David thanks God for:

- His Rescue (v. 10)—He struck down the firstborn of Israel
- His Power (vv. 11–13)—He divided the Red Sea
- His Presence (v. 16)—He led His people through the wilderness
- His Provision (v. 25)—He gives food to all flesh
- His Creation (vv. 5–9)—He created the earth, the sun, the moon, the stars.
- His Protection (vv. 17–21)—He struck down the kings who opposed Israel as they traveled to the Promised Land.

Let's build grateful hearts. Rooted in the steadfast love of

God, let's build hearts of thankfulness that testify to the world of God's beauty, goodness, and majesty. It is a process. It takes time. Let's build one prayer of thanksgiving at a time.

Chapter Sixty-One
HIS DESIRE

> *...Let us run with endurance the race that is set before us, looking to Jesus, the founder and perfecter of our faith, who for the joy that was set before him endured the cross, despising the shame, and is seated at the right hand of the throne of God.*
> Hebrews 12:1b–2

I love to watch my young nephew with my brother, his dad. He thinks his dad is the greatest thing on earth and absolutely worships him. No matter what my brother is doing, whether it's fixing something, playing a video game, sleeping on the couch, driving in the truck, or mowing the grass, his son wants to be right next to him. His greatest joy and delight is to be right next to his dad.

The first few verses of Mark 3 are some of my favorites in all of Scripture because we get a glimpse into the desire and delight of Jesus here. Mark 3:13–14 reads:

> *And he (Jesus) went up on the mountain and **called to him those whom he desired,** and they came to him. And he appointed twelve (whom he also named apostles) **so that they might be with him** and he might send them out to preach.*

Just as my brother's presence brings deep joy to my nephew, your existence delights the Godhead! When God created the universe, he thought about you! Like the disciples, the call for you to come to Christ is entirely born out of the desire and delight of Jesus. He wants you.

The Scriptures teach us that God lacks nothing; he has no deficiency in himself. The Creator of the universe needs nothing from us (Acts 17:24–25). Yet, he pursues us. He loves us. He wants to be with us.

Sometimes this is hard to believe. The experiences of our lives herald the opposite message. We haven't felt wanted, desired, or delighted in. Words like abandon, ugly, awkward, and broken play on repeat in our hearts.

The idea that Someone would actually long to be with us is foreign and improbable. Keenly aware of our sin, weakness, failure, and imperfections, it's hard for us to imagine being the object of Someone's delight and desire. But, Jesus isn't like us. His love is perfect and His forgiveness is complete.

Sister, today feast on what is true. The One who made you, the One who knows everything about you, the One who is perfect in love and hope, wants you. You are a delight to his heart. You bring him joy. It pleased him to create you.

And he went to great lengths to make this fellowship and friendship possible. Jesus endured the pain and shame of the cross so that he might be with you and you might be with Him.

Let this objective fact overwhelm your subjective thoughts. His perfect sacrifice guarantees his commitment to and love for you. Remember that he initiated this relationship with you, he secured it by his death and resurrection, and he delights in it. His joy and desire is to call you close so that you might be with him. Mind-blowing, I know. But, utterly true!

Chapter Sixty-Two
KINDNESS & REPENTANCE

*For God has done what the law, weakened by the flesh, could not do. By sending his own Son in the likeness of sinful flesh and for sin, he condemned sin in the flesh in order that the righteous requirement of the law **might be fulfilled in us**, who walk not according to the flesh but according to the Spirit*
Romans 8:3—4

In an article recalling heart-warming stories of 2020, I read about a Muslim immigrant who was running for Congress in Virginia. Sadly, during his campaign, he received deeply hurtful anti-Muslim tweets from a conservative Virginia man. Horrible lies were spread on social media.

Despite these terribly insulting remarks, the attacked man did not respond in anger or with hate. On the contrary, when the politician found out that the insulter and his wife were struggling with medical debt, he made a donation to help cover his attacker's medical expenses. His kindness prompted an apology from the aggressor and initiated a friendship between the two men.

Few people would have blamed the politician if he responded to the deep insults inflicted on him with bitterness or anger. His outrage would have been justified and understandable. Indeed, no one would have expected him to repay such evil with grace and goodness.

And yet he did. He responded with mercy and his kindness led to his enemy's repentance and friendship.

In an even deeper and much more beautiful way, Jesus has responded to our rebellion, disobedience, insults, and even our indifference with extravagant grace and mercy.

The Bible teaches:

> *None is righteous; no, not one; no one understands; no one seeks God. All have turned aside; together they have become worthless; no one does good, not even one. Their throat is an open grave; they use their tongues to deceive. The venom of asps is under their lips. Their mouth is full of curses and bitterness.* (Romans 3:10–14)

This is the reality of humanity apart from God's grace. Therefore, God is absolutely just in his wrath against mankind. We are his enemies by our own choice; we rebel against his holiness. Our hearts continually wander away from him, going our own way, refusing to submit to his law. Just like the Virginia constituent, we heap insults. We fully deserve punishment for our sin.

But, the Gospel heralds a different story! Out of his crazy love and mercy, instead of condemning us as we deserve, our Father poured out his fierce and justified wrath on his very own Son **so that** the righteous requirement that the Law demanded would be fulfilled in us! We are **the recipients of God's righteousness!** In fact, we are credited with the perfect obedience of Christ even though we are the ones who deserved condemnation!

He has taken our condemnation and offered us, in return, his perfection. What extravagant kindness. This kindness leads us to repentance and friendship. What an awesome God we have!

Chapter Sixty-Three
FACE TO FACE

No longer will there be anything accursed, but the throne of God and of the Lamb will be in it, and his servants will worship him. They will see his face, and his name will be on their foreheads. And night will be no more. They will need no light of lamp or sun, for the Lord God will be their light, and they will reign forever and ever.
Revelation 22:3–5

A kindergarten teacher at our church shared the sweetest story about two of her precious students. For the entire 2020–2021 school year, two boys only ever saw each other over the computer screen. Their classes were only online from September through June.

Despite the physical distance, these classmates became good friends. While they enjoyed each other virtually, their friendship was incomplete at best. The fullness of their relationship wasn't realized until they saw each other face to face. So when the day came for the kindergarteners to receive their certificates of completion in person, a beautiful expression of affection radiated from these friends.

They called out for one another, raced towards each other and vigorously embraced. Both were filled with a long-awaited happiness. As the teachers witnessed the emotional encounter, they were deeply moved by the innocence and joy of this exchange.

When my friend shared that story with us, I immediately thought about the day when we will meet Jesus face to face. Right now, we only see dimly (1 Corinthians 13:12), but one day we will stand face to face with the One who knows us better than we know ourselves and loves us more than we could ever dare to dream! The warmth of his smile and the love in his eyes will penetrate our souls. We will touch the nail-pierced scars on his hands. We will hear the roar of his contagious laughter. And we will know and experience a fullness of joy like we never could imagine.

BUT, there's more to this amazing encounter. Sisters, **it will be such a great and deep joy for him to see you too** (Hebrews 12:2)! Doesn't that blow your mind? He will be so delighted to see **YOU** face to face too! We know that this is the heart of the Father towards us because Jesus taught us that when the Father saw his rebellious, selfish, squandering child coming home, the Scriptures say:

> *But while he* [the rebellious child] *was still a long way off, his father saw him and felt compassion and ran and embraced him and kissed him.* (Luke 15:20)

Face to face. You will see him face to face. What a glorious day that will be. May the anticipated delight of that day infuse your heart with hope and joy today.

> "There are far, far better things ahead than any we leave behind."
> —*C.S. Lewis*

Chapter Sixty-Four
BECOMING YOUR PARENT

"For those whom he foreknew he also predestined to be conformed to the image of his Son in order that he might be the firstborn among many brothers."
Romans 8:29

The Progressive Insurance Company's "Unbecoming Your Parents" commercials are hysterical. Whether the ad highlights going to the movies, shopping for clothes, or decorating the house, they make me laugh out loud.

Many of us can probably relate to this idea of becoming our parents. Something comes out of our mouths, and we think, "That is exactly something my mother would say." Or we'll respond to a certain situation and know, "I get that from my dad."

We aren't intentionally trying to be like our parents, it just happens. Somewhere along the way, what they say (and even how they say it) has just become a part of who we are… like it or not.

How does that happen? How do we end up becoming our

parents? There are probably very well-articulated, deep, psychological reasons behind the answers to those questions. You won't find that here.

Perhaps though, our parents' thoughts, mannerisms, and phrases seep out of us because we spent a ton of time together. We've heard their antidotes and clichés (or outbursts) a thousand times and so one day, unexpectedly, those words exit our lips too. Unbeknownst to us, years of time together and day after day of a shared life deeply formed who we are. Words, thoughts, actions, and habits slowly got woven into the fabric of our being. Sometimes, we like it and sometimes we don't.

However, contrary to the comical Progressive Insurance commercials, as Christ Followers, we are **called to become like our parent**. Romans 8:29 says,*"For those whom he foreknew **he also predestined to be conformed to the image of his Son....**"* Hebrews 1:3 tells us that in becoming like Christ, we are becoming like our heavenly Father for Christ is the exact picture of who the Father is. We are called to become like our parent.

While the Scriptures teach us that it is the Holy Spirit who works to form Christ in us, ***how*** does this happen? How does he do it? How does the Spirit cause us to become like our Father and reflect the image of His Son?

Perhaps, in much the same way that the habits and thoughts of our earthly parents are formed in us by virtue of time spent together, as we spend time with our heavenly Father, hearing His thoughts and words over and over again, seeing his character on display through his Word and in the Body of Christ, the Spirit conforms us to the image of Jesus. Perhaps our communion with Him, through prayer and the Scriptures, is the means by which the Spirit changes us.

Father, give us both the desire and the drive to spend time with you. As we abide in you and you in us, transform us into the image of your Son that we might reflect your goodness and glory to the world.

Chapter Sixty-Five
COME OUT OF HIDING

*By this we shall know that we are of the truth and
reassure our heart before him; for whenever our heart condemns us,
God is greater than our heart, and he knows everything.*
1 John 3:19–20

Last week, my mom and I were looking through my great-grandmother's old recipe box. Buried amongst the instructions for cookies and soups was an old yellowed newspaper clipping, an Ann Landers letter entitled, "Breakdown Patient Cannot Cure Self." What pierced me was that she carefully and secretly hid this tiny article in a place where no one would find it.

My Gram did, in fact, have a nervous breakdown and was committed, for a time, to an institution. However, mental illness wasn't discussed or treated in the early 70s the way it is today. It broke my heart that in her darkest days, she needed to hide her struggle.

While I am grateful that our society has made enormous

progress in admitting and addressing hard issues over the last several decades, we often still hide.

We hide in our shame. We hide in our anxiety. We hide in our weakness. We hide in our sin. We hide in our fear. Though we long to be fully known and truly loved, we are terrified of rejection, rehearsing in our heads, "If they knew that about me, they would not want anything to do with me."

Sisters, here is good news for us! Your Father knows everything about you—every dark secret, every embarrassing thought, every evil desire. And still—**he is for you**! Nothing in all of creation (including your darkest moments of shame, fear, and doubt) can separate you from the love God has for you in Christ (Romans 8). Nothing! Dear One, he knows it and he still chooses you and always will. He will never change his mind about you. Because of Jesus, he has fully forgiven and accepted you as his beloved daughter. You bring him joy!

So, come out of hiding. Walk into the light. Run to Jesus! For in him, the freedom and the joy and the hope that your heart so desperately longs for (and perhaps doesn't dare to believe could really exist) is waiting for you!

Chapter Sixty-Six
BUILDING A KINGDOM

So then you are no longer strangers and aliens, but you are fellow citizens with the saints and members of the household of God, built on the foundation of the apostles and prophets, Christ Jesus himself being the cornerstone, in whom the whole structure, being joined together, grows into a holy temple in the Lord. In him you also are being built together into a dwelling place for God by the Spirit.
Ephesians 2:19–22

When our family first arrived at our current church, we desperately longed to meet people and connect. We hungered for community and friendship in our new church home. But, it was difficult.

Our church is big and sometimes it's easy to feel lost or even invisible. It was challenging for us to find our place. Maybe you've felt that way too.

Out of our desperation, my husband and I calculated a multifaceted strategy. First, we parked ourselves in the exact same seats every week. We figured that if we sat in the same place every Sunday, at least the other people who repeatedly chose that section would notice us. Second, every week we attended a different Sunday school class. We supposed that we were bound to find relatable people in one of those classes.

Like I said, we were desperate for community. While our strategy worked to some degree, the most meaningful connections occurred when we began to serve. Serving alongside other believers fosters unity, community, friendship, and beauty.

When God's chosen people were exiled in Babylon, Nehemiah was serving in the court of King Artaxerxes, and he learned that Jerusalem lay in ruins (Nehemiah 1). Nehemiah prayed and then courageously approached the king to ask for permission to return to Jerusalem and rebuild it (Nehemiah 2). By God's sovereign and gracious hand, the king granted his request and Nehemiah and many other Jews returned to Jerusalem to repair the wall.

The third chapter of the book describes construction specifications—from the names of those rebuilding the wall, to the precise locations of their efforts, to the precise details of their labor. But here is what strikes me: everyone (except the nobles, and that's a story for a different day) aided in the rebuilding.

- The priests repaired the wall.
- The officials repaired the wall.
- The goldsmiths repaired the wall.
- The perfumers repaired the wall.
- The rulers repaired the wall.
- The daughters repaired the wall.
- The Levites repaired the wall.
- The temple servants repaired the wall.
- The merchants repaired the wall.

EVERYONE worked together. Everyone served. Everyone got their hands dirty.

What a beautiful picture of the people of God! Repairing a wall wasn't the giftedness or skillset of the goldsmiths, but they shared in the labor. Repairing a wall wasn't the passion of the perfumers, but they shared in the labor. They shared in the labor because they were building something together that was bigger and better than what any one person could do alone.

Sisters, we share in the same privilege! In Christ, we are building a kingdom, his glorious eternal Kingdom. Sometimes we serve in ways that directly line up with our gifts and passions. Sometimes we just join in and build the wall. But, we're all called to serve.

And in that joint serving, there is unity and beauty. Is there an area where God might be nudging your heart today? Is there an area where God is calling you to step out of your comfort zone and serve? Listen to that still small voice. What a joy it is for us to serve together and partner in the Gospel!

Chapter Sixty-Seven
HE GIVES MORE

Jesus turned, and seeing her he said, "Take heart, daughter; your faith has made you well."
Matthew 9:22

He said to her, "Daughter, your faith has healed you. Go in peace and be freed from your suffering."
Mark 5:34

While Jesus traveled with his disciples one day, a desperate synagogue ruler knelt before the Messiah and begged him to heal his dying daughter. Moved with compassion, the Miracle Worker follows the heartsick dad.

However, while on the way, an anguished woman interrupted their journey. In the midst of the thronging crowd surrounding Jesus, she pressed her way through to him, touched the fringe of his garment, and then disappeared into the commotion, hoping to remain unnoticed.

But, she got caught.

At the moment she touched him, she's healed. Jesus knows that power has gone out from him, and he immediately stops, asking who touched him. The woman, knowing she can no longer remain invisible, trembled before Jesus and fell at his feet.

Here's what I love about this story: this once-despairing woman was content with what she received. For her, the physical healing was sufficient. She attempted to quickly sneak in and slip out of the crowd. That's understandable. She had been hopelessly sick and barred from society for so long. We get it. For her, it is enough.

But not for Jesus.

He wasn't satisfied; he wanted to give her more. Yes, he healed her. Yes, he stopped her bleeding. But he wanted to offer her more, so much more.

First of all, he saw her and he wanted her to know it. For years, she had been unseen, unnoticed, invisible. But then, everything changed. She had been seen; she mattered to him and he ensured that she knew it.

He made eye contact with her and took time to speak personally to her. Though Jesus was attending to a very important leader's emergency, he paused and singled her out of the demanding crowd. He saw her.

Second, he gave her a new identity. He called her "daughter." She belonged to him now, a member of his family, and he wanted her and everyone else there to realize it. She has a new name.

Finally, he sends her in peace. No longer were shame and hiding her defining markers. She was both personally and publicly restored. ***He gave her so much more than what she asked for.***

Sister, what does your heart long for? Is it to know that you belong? You do. You are his, and you have been grafted into a family that is bigger and better than you could imagine. Do you long to know that he sees you? He does. You are not invisible to him, and you never escape his care. Are you dreaming for freedom but instead are carrying a heavy load of shame? Sister, you are free. You are a new creation—the old has gone, the new has come. Do you need restoration? Remember, a new day is coming, a better day. This is a guarantee.

Wherever you are today, know that the heart of the Father towards you is far more loving and good than you can even imagine!

Chapter Sixty-Eight
IMITATION CRAB MEAT

I am the true vine, and my Father is the vinedresser.
John 15:1

Maryland has always been my home. I was born here and raised here, with the exception of my few college years. I am a Maryland girl through and through.

Therefore, it almost goes without saying that I love steamed crabs. In fact, I pretty much love all things crab: crab dip, crab cakes, crab soup, crab imperial... you name it with the word "crab" in it, and I'll eat it.

However, I am also quite picky about my crabs and can identify imitation crab meat in one bite!

In John 15, Jesus talked with his disciples prior to his death in what is called the Farewell Discourse. The Master Teacher often used simple word pictures to help his followers understand deep truths. As his death and earthly departure were imminent, the future of his disciples weighed heavy on his heart.

What did he want them to remember most? What did he

choose as some of his last words to them? What instructions did he give them?

He reminded his disciples of who he was, the True Vine. He is where life is found. He is the One who produces fruit in them (Galatians 5:22–23). Apart from Him, they can do nothing.

His urgent call was for his friends to remain in him, to abide in the True Vine. Wasn't it interesting that Jesus says that he is the ***True*** Vine? Why not just say "the vine"? What was he driving at?

The word "true" reminds us that in this world there are imitation vines. There are vines that have the appearance of giving life; but in reality, they offer no nourishment to the branch. There are vines that are fakes.

As we consider the word "true," questions come up: What are the imitation vines in my life? Where do I seek life and nourishment apart from Jesus himself? Where am I trying to produce fruit on my own, apart from the vine?

Imitation vines fail. Life and nourishment for the soul are only found in Christ. Trying to produce fruit apart from the Vine is not only an effort in futility, but it is also utterly exhausting.

Jesus' words bring comfort and hope. As we abide in him, he promises that he will produce fruit in us. As we abide in him, he promises that he will pour his joy into our hearts (John 15:11). As we abide in him, the Father is glorified. The invitation is there: come and abide. Remain in the True Vine. The Father delights to bring life and nourishment to your soul.

Chapter Sixty-Nine
JUST GET HERE

Therefore encourage one another and build one another up, just as you are doing... And we urge you, brothers, admonish the idle, encourage the faint-hearted, help the weak, be patient with them all. See that no one repays anyone evil for evil, but always seek to do good to one another and to everyone.
1 Thessalonians 5:11, 14–15

Recently my husband and I joined a gym together. I've never been a fan of going to the gym; I don't enjoy lifting weights and usually feel intimidated and weak surrounded by machines I don't know how to use.

However, the trainers at our new fitness center implore us, "Just get here and we'll take care of the rest." They firmly believe that getting there is the hardest part.

Once we arrive, they determine to take over. It's their job to motivate, encourage, and lead apathetic members towards better physical health.

And they do! From the second we enter the door, they inspire us to work hard. They push us to do more than we think we are capable of achieving, cheer for us by name, and don't let us get away with cheating on our reps. They are for us, and we know it. Their encouragement leads to our flourishing.

This community of gym rats is a sweet, though far less glorious, picture of the Body of Believers. In his infinite love and wisdom, the Father determined that for us to flourish and accomplish His kingdom's purpose, we need a community. We are not to walk alone. He has given us each other that we might encourage, inspire, cheer for, and hold one another accountable.

Some days, it's all I can do to just get to the gym. I don't have it in me to push myself out of my comfort zone or to work hard. Left to myself, I'd honestly rather sit on the couch and eat junk food.

That's why I need my coach. That's why I need my team members. I can't do it by myself.

Some days, I'm all in. I'm energized and ready to go. That's when the team needs me.

Sister, you need community. And your community needs you. Throughout the Scriptures, God exhorts us repeatedly to live in community.

- To love one another in community
- To be devoted to one another in community
- To build each other up in community
- To forgive one another in community
- To admonish one another in community
- To serve one another in community
- To submit to one another in community

My father-in-law often preached, "There are no Lone Ranger Christians. Even the Lone Ranger has Tonto."

Where are you today? Do you need some extra encouragement? Are you feeling isolated and lonely in your faith? Pursue community. Are you on fire for the Lord today? Are you enjoying the richness of his blessings and goodness? Your community needs you.

Community isn't easy. There are days when I want to throw the medicine ball right at my trainer's head. But, community is worth it, and you need it. The hardest part is taking the first step. Trust that God knows what he is doing. Trust that his ways are best. Trust that community is what you need. Trust that your community will be life and health for your soul. Like my coach says, "Just get here. We'll take care of the rest."

Chapter Seventy
FRONT ROW SEATS

When the master of the feast tasted the water now become wine, and did not know where it came from (though the servants who had drawn the water knew), the master of the feast called the bridegroom and said to him, "Everyone serves the good wine first, and when people have drunk freely, then the poor wine. But you have kept the good wine until now."
John 2:9-10

In 2021, GQ magazine published an article chronicling the most expensive sporting tickets of all time. Court-side tickets to an NBA game sold for over $150,000. The MLB World Series reported tickets for the best seats went for over $1.5 million!

Obviously, your average spectator isn't shelling out this kind of money to watch the game; but some fans are! Why? Why would anyone spend such an insane amount of cash on a game? Why? Because front-row seats are amazing! Being inches away from the action is a thrill. Experiencing a sporting contest, a

Broadway show, or a music concert up close is unforgettable. But it's often reserved only for the elite.

John 2 records Jesus' first miracle, the Wedding at Cana. John tells us that at some point during the matrimonial festivities, the party runs out of wine. So Mary calls on her eldest son to make things right (moms are really good at calling on first-born sons to help out).

Jesus obeys and instructs the house's servants to fill six large (20 to 30 gallons each) purification jars with water. After filling the jars with plain old water, he says to them, *"Now draw some out and take it to the master of the feast"* (John 2:8).

Imagine for a moment that you are one of the servants. What are you thinking? Are you terrified of what your master will do to you when you bring him this water? Are you afraid that your master will be embarrassed in front of his guests when his servants bring him water? Will you lose your job? Will you be beaten? Will something worse happen?

Remember, Jesus does not yet have the reputation of being a miracle worker. To them, he is just an average guy, another normal guest at the wedding.

We know the story. Amazingly, the water became wine, and not just any wine but really good wine. It is a crazy, fantastic, awesome inauguration of the miraculous signs Jesus will perform throughout his ministry.

But, what is utterly astonishing, is that Jesus chooses to reveal his first miracle to the lowest of the low. It isn't the elite who have a front-row seat to his glory; it's the invisible ones. The servants. The most unnoticed at the party. It isn't the master, and it isn't the bridegroom. It isn't the wealthiest most prominent family in attendance. It's the servants.

This is the heart of Jesus. He is for those who are unseen. He delights in mesmerizing the unknown. The marginalized. The weak. The outcast.

I like to imagine this scene as if it was a Hollywood movie. When the master tasted the wine and praised the bridegroom, did the servants immediately turn and look at Jesus? Did Jesus smile at them? Did he wink at them, like two people who are in on a secret together? Did they become his first followers? Were they noticed by Someone important for the first time in their life?

Whether you feel like the bridegroom or the servant today, remember that Jesus delights to mesmerize you with his goodness and his power. He sees you. He knows you. You have a front-row seat to his Presence. Today, let his winemaking remind you of his heart for you.

Chapter Seventy-One
CONTAGIOUS WORSHIP

Oh, magnify the LORD with me, and let us exalt his name together.
Psalm 34:3

Let the word of Christ dwell in you richly, teaching and admonishing one another in all wisdom, singing psalms and hymns and spiritual songs, with thankfulness in your hearts to God.
Colossians 3:16

Several years ago, my husband took me to watch the Baltimore Ravens play the Indianapolis Colts. While I don't share his love for football, he was excited for me to experience the thrill of a live game. When we arrived at the stadium, it was bitter cold. Strike one.

When we approached the front gate, I saw that bags (of which I had a considerable size) were not permitted inside the arena. Of course, my husband didn't know this because he never carries a purse. The car was far away and so because it was just a cheap drawstring bag, I had to throw it away.

Therefore, as we made our way to our seats (in the freezing cold), I lumbered with all of the contents of my discarded bag. Strike two.

Finally, we reached our seats, and they were fantastic. But when we found our spots, he told me that fans don't really sit at all during the game. What? Are you kidding me? You mean I am going to stand, in the freezing cold, holding a plethora of necessary items, without a bag, for 3 1/2 hours? Strike three.

Then the game started.

The place erupted! Loud music blared, and I couldn't hear myself think. Crazy fans cheered and high-fived me all over our chaotic section. Baltimore's star defender danced and performed his traditional pre-game show.

Just like that, I was all in. It was electric and infectious, and I felt so connected to my fellow Ravens fans. I was part of the team; the excitement captured me. In that moment, I became a worshiper of black and purple.

Worship is contagious. At a football game or at church. Within the walls of the stadium, the intensity and frenzy of the football game inspires awe among its spectators.

In an even more miraculous and powerful way, the Holy Spirit ignites passion and vitality in the gathering of the saints for corporate worship. He uses the worship of others to inspire us and draw us in. Throughout the Bible, the people of God are called to gather together for worship. We feed off the love and affection of others.

Where are you today? Do you want your heart to be ignited with zeal for the Lord? Do you hunger to worship in spirit and truth, with outrageous joy and abandon? Is corporate worship a priority in your life?

Sister, our hearts were created for worship. Glorious, transformative worship ignites in community. Worship is contagious. Magnify the Lord with me.

Chapter Seventy-Two

FRONT PORCH PRESENTS

For his invisible attributes, namely, his eternal power and divine nature, have been clearly perceived, ever since the creation of the world, in the things that have been made. So they are without excuse.
Romans 1:20

For we are his workmanship, created in Christ Jesus for good works, which God prepared beforehand, that we should walk in them.
Ephesians 2:10

Our cat frequently leaves us presents on the front porch. One particular morning, the successful hunt resulted in a prize (well, it was actually only half a prize) on the back deck. Soon after his deposit, my husband removed the victim of Obie's morning chase and discarded it in our pasture, about fifty yards from the house.

A few hours later, that mutilated half bunny (sorry to all you cottontail lovers) reappeared on the deck! Now, I don't know enough about animal psychology to tell you why our cat did this, but we were mystified and (I'll admit) slightly humored that he delivered that rabbit a second time.

Why does a cat bring his treasure to the porch? Why does he retrieve it again after it's been discarded? How did he find it? Why did he do it? What is going on in his mind?

I have absolutely no idea what the answers to those questions are. But, the mystery of the returning prize reminds me of how incredibly creative our God is. He forms bewildering creatures with peculiar habits in a fascinating world filled with wonder, beauty, and awe.

Beauty and creativity are celebrated by God. His glorious nature is revealed in what he has made (Romans 1:20). ***Likewise, creativity is engrained deeply within each of us because we are made in the image of our wonderful Creator.***

As his image bearers, the Father entrusts each one of us with creative work to carry out. Meaningful work. Beautiful, imaginative, and unique work. It doesn't matter if you are a student or if you are retired, if you work as a CEO, or if you are a stay-at-home mom. If you belong to Christ, he has good works that he has prepared in advance for you. Works of creativity and beauty. Works that reflect his goodness and glory.

Sometimes we limit creativity to art and music. But, the act of creating stretches far beyond the boundaries we assign. For some of us, God calls us to create the warmth and welcome of the gospel by opening our homes to friends and neighbors. Some of us are designed to create safe places for hard conversations at work or at home. Some of us create revolutionary technology in the areas of science and industry. How are you gifted creatively? What do you enjoy creating? Where is God calling you to display his goodness and beauty in the world? Have you ever considered that in doing these things you actually image your Creator?

Today, as you go about your day, be creative!

Chapter Seventy-Three
STILL INVITED

So when they had come together, they asked him, "Lord, will you at this time restore the kingdom of Israel?" He said to them, "It is not for you to know times or seasons that the Father has fixed by his own authority. But you will receive power when the Holy Spirit comes upon you, and you will be my witnesses in Jerusalem and in all Judea and Samaria, and to the end of the earth."
Acts 1:6–8

One of the most humiliating moments of my life occurred at a friend's outdoor wedding reception. Beautiful white tents spread across the manicured green lawn. Lace-covered tables adorned with garden-fresh flowers outlined the  afternoon festivities. It was a magnificent display of elegance and grace.

Until it wasn't.

As I was returning from the lovely buffet back to my assigned table, I accidentally (and not so gracefully) tripped over the very well-hidden cord that connects the top of the tent to the stabilizing peg buried in the ground. The tent catastrophically collapsed. The tranquility of the day was violently disrupted. Annoyed guests glared at me. My face burned with embarrassment. I was mortified.

Thankfully, the bride quickly approached. She assured me that my mishap did not ruin her day. She kindly (yet unsuccessfully) attempted to convince me that not that many people witnessed the debacle. She refused to let me run away and hide. She had invited me to this celebration and even though I caused quite a disturbing scene, I was still invited.

In our passage today, the disciples, though they have spent three years with Jesus, still ask the wrong questions. They are misdirected in their focus and unclear about his mission. Even after witnessing his death and resurrection, they still don't get it.

But Jesus isn't frustrated or discouraged by them. He doesn't throw in the towel with these guys. Despite all the reasons why they **SHOULD** get this by now, he still invites them to be a part of his Great Mission to the world! He doesn't give up on them. He doesn't cast them away and start over with a new group of smarter, more committed guys. Rather, he uses them to bring the Gospel to the uttermost parts of the world!

I don't know about you, but I am so thankful that he doesn't give up on us—even and especially when we should get it by now. Not only is he patient and kind with us, but he invites us to partner with him on his Great Mission to rescue the world. Despite all of our weaknesses and sins and all the times we leave disaster in our wake, he still invites us to participate with him in the glorious story of redemption. What an amazing Savior we have!

Chapter Seventy-Four
IT ALL ENDS WELL

Let every person be subject to the governing authorities.
For there is no authority except from God,
and those that exist have been instituted by God.
Romans 13:1

Our God is in the heavens; he does all that he pleases.
Psalm 115:3

At a world-famous theme park, there is a wonderful African safari attraction. This ride simulates an open-sided ride through the savanna of East Africa. For a brief moment at one point on the  adventure, the bridge over which the cruiser crosses feigns collapse. In the water below, man-eating hippos threaten harm. Young children gasp and grab the safety bar as adults chuckle. Seasoned tourists know that the ride is safe, that they will reach their destination, and there is no reason to be alarmed.

Tensions surrounding politics permeate the news. You don't have to search long on a social media feed to uncover articles, comments, and videos relating to domestic and international governmental problems. In election seasons, we feel stress. Important issues divide families. Hostility elevates at work. Emotions rage. Friendships are strained. In its various forms, fear invades our souls.

While believers are called to honor those in authority over us and submit to our leadership, we remind ourselves that we need not fear even when chaos surrounds us. No matter which side wins or loses, we have reason to be at peace.

Just like the seasoned riders on the amusement park attraction know that the ride will end well, we too have confidence that all will be made right in the end. Nothing happens in our country apart from the sovereign and loving hand of our God. Nothing! No party rises without his consent. No bill is passed apart from his notice.

Therefore, we can rest. Our trust and our confidence are in Him, not in any system that people create.

So where are you today? Is your heart restless? Are you struggling because the future seems so uncertain? Does the state of our country cause you to lose sleep?

Sister, your God is in control. He always has been, and he always will be. Nothing happens apart from or outside of his good and sovereign power. May this reality bring peace to our troubled hearts.

Chapter Seventy-Five
THE STORY'S AUTHOR

> *Your eyes saw my unformed substance; in your book were written, every one of them, the days that were formed for me, when as yet there was none of them.*
> Psalm 139:16

The Broadway musical *Wicked* is the story of how the Wicked Witch of the West (from the *Wizard of Oz*) becomes that very person. Elphaba (that's her name) wasn't always the evil sorceress we come to know in the movie.

As the musical unfolds, the audience learns how her family relationships, circumstances, and friendships impact and form her, particularly her best friend relationship with Glinda (the Good Witch from the *Wizard of Oz*). It's heartwarming and tragic, beautiful and sad.

Wicked reminds us that everyone has a story, a story that is full of triumphs and tragedies, one that is ever-changing and often unknown to most. Relationships and circumstances mold and shape us into the people we are today.

Some of those memories are full of joy and triumph; some of pain and heartache. How do we make sense of our stories? How do we reconcile tragedy and triumph? How do we embrace the story in which we find ourselves?

I only know one way. We remember that our story has an Author—and he is good.

- **God is the Author of every story:** *"You saw me before I was born and scheduled each day of my life before I began to breathe. Every day was recorded in your book!"* (Psalm 139:16)
- **God is always good:** *"The LORD is good to all, and his mercy is over all that he has made."* (Psalm 145:9)
- **God is sovereign over every detail of creation:** *"I am God, and there is none like me, declaring the end from the beginning and from ancient times things not yet done, saying, 'My counsel shall stand, and I will accomplish all my purpose.'"* (Isaiah 46:9b–10)
- **God always has a purpose in the pain:** *"And we know that for those who love God all things work together for good, for those who are called according to his purpose."* (Romans 8:28)
- **Joy is coming:** *"And the ransomed of the Lord shall return and come to Zion with singing; everlasting joy shall be upon their heads; they shall obtain gladness and joy, and sorrow and sighing shall flee away."* (Isaiah 35:10)
- **God will make all things beautiful:** *"He has made everything beautiful in its time."* (Ecclesiastes 3:11a)

Maybe you are struggling to believe these truths. Welcome to the club.

In the midst of suffering and heartache, it's really hard to trust in the truth of God's Word. Let me reassure your heart (and mine) today.

It is not the strength of your faith that makes these truths real. It is not the strength of your faith that keeps you in the love and favor of God. ***It is God's unchangeable nature on which we bank our hope.*** It is God's unwavering commitment to you (and to me) that is our anchor. Even in your doubt and wrestling, he will never change! Wherever you are today, Sister, may you remember that your story, with all its highs and lows, is a marvelous one that God is writing with purpose and beauty.

Chapter Seventy-Six
TENNIS SHOES

For I the LORD do not change; therefore you,
O children of Jacob are not consumed.
Malachi 3:6

Jesus Christ is the same yesterday and today and forever.
Hebrews 13:8

My son recently purchased a new pair of Reeboks. When he showed me his choice, I laughed out loud saying, "I wore those exact same shoes when I was in middle school."

His reply was, "Yeah. Now they're retro." It's amusing (and sometimes baffling to me) how the same styles keep coming back. Who decides these things? Who decides when big hair is cool again? Who decides when baggy jeans are "in" again? Who decides when my grandmother's shoes are the latest rage?

Fashion styles always change; fads come and then quickly

disappear. The trends of previous decades, even the ones you hoped would never reemerge, resurface time and time again. In the world of fashion, change is inevitable.

But really, change is everywhere; it is certainly not limited to the world of fashion. In a day where change is constant, our never-changing God is a fortress for our souls. No matter how much culture or people or the environment changes, our Father is unchanging.

This attribute of God is called immutability. **God is unchanging in his covenant, will, and promises.** God was, and is, and always will be the same. He is forever sovereign over every detail of creation. He is good in all his ways, in every moment, for all eternity. He is unalterably just; his ways are always right and perfect and pure.

When the storms of life roll in, our hearts need an anchor.

- When right is called wrong and wrong is celebrated, God is sovereign, good, and just.
- When a trusted friend betrays you, God is sovereign, good, and just.
- When the cancer comes back, God is sovereign, good, and just.
- When I unexpectedly lose my job, God is sovereign, good, and just.
- When my child walks a path of self-destruction and I feel helpless, God is sovereign, good, and just.
- When caring for aging parents overwhelms you, God is sovereign, good, and just.
- When anxiety is a constant companion, God is sovereign, good, and just.
- When addiction is winning, God is sovereign, good, and just.

Sister, where are you today? How would you fill in this blank

When_____, God is sovereign, good, and just.

Life is full of storms. Some roll in outside of our control, and others are a product of our own doing. Regardless, in the chaos and change of life, our God remains the same, and therefore he can be trusted. Put your hope in him—he will never fail. In fact, he cannot fail because he never changes.

Chapter Seventy-Seven

ONE WORD CHANGES EVERYTHING

*"Death and life are in the power of the tongue,
and those who love it will eat its fruits."*
Proverbs 18:21

Words are powerful. Recently, a photographer posted two pictures of the same person side by side. After the first photo was snapped, the artist declared, "You're beautiful."

The second picture was then shot. The transformation is unmistakable! In the latter image smiles replace frowns, bright eyes expel sadness, and a noticeable joy emerges on the models' faces.

One word changes everything.

How might your heart (and face) lift if an encouraging word is spoken to you today? How might your mind transform if the truest and most promising declarations, the affirmations you most long to hear, are spoken to you today?

- What if I told you that the Creator and Sustainer of the entire universe says that *you are the apple of his eye* (Psalm 17:8)? He thinks about you. He adores you. He sacrificed his life so you could be his forever.
- What if I told you that God knows every single dark corner of your heart and still says that *he likes you and chooses you* to be His (Psalm 139)?
- What if I told you that *a place, beyond your wildest dreams*, is being prepared right now for you, and the Lover of your soul is coming back to get you and take you there with joy (John 14)?
- What if I told you that one day there will be *no more crying, no more pain, no more mourning, no more death* (Revelation 21)?
- What if I told you that every single detail of your life is being loving and sovereignly guided and directed by the One who cares more for you than you could ever imagine (Ephesians 1:11)?

What if the answers to these questions grounded our thinking? What if our souls were anchored to these truths instead of the circumstances surrounding us? What if the words of life replaced the fears, failures and insecurities that run on repeat in our minds? What if our hearts were tuned to the whisper of the Savior, the One who says, "You are beautiful, for I have made you mine."

Today, let your heart, mind, and soul feast on these words that your God joyfully declares over you:

*Now to him who is able to **keep you from stumbling** and to **present you blameless** before the presence of his glory **with great joy**, to the only God, our Savior, through Jesus Christ our Lord, be glory, majesty, dominion, and authority, before all time and now and forever. Amen.*
Jude 24–25

Chapter Seventy-Eight
HEY BABE!

Jesus said to her, "Woman, why are you weeping? Whom are you seeking?" Supposing him to be the gardener, she said to him, "Sir, if you have carried him away, tell me where you have laid him, and I will take him away." Jesus said to her, "Mary." She turned and said to him in Aramaic, "Rabboni!" (which means Teacher).
John 20:15–16

Since my dad died, I have been surprised about what I miss the most about him.

I miss hearing the quirky way he used goofy words that he created (although he truly thought they were real words).

I miss the way he would stop by my house, unannounced, just to chit-chat.

I miss the way he would look at me as if I could do no wrong. But, probably what I miss the most are two words: "Hey Babe!"

Ever since I was a little girl, my dad's most familiar address to me was, "Hey Babe!" In the days before caller ID and cell phones, his "Hey Babe!" instantly identified the voice on the other end of the line. When I walked into the room, "Hey Babe!" were the first words out of his mouth.

Even at the end, when his strength failed, he'd whisper "Hey Babe" from his hospital bed. No one has called me that since, and no one may ever call me "Babe" again.

In John 20, we find Mary Magdalene bereft with grief and weeping at the tomb of Jesus. She has come to anoint his body with spices to complete the burial preparations. To her horror, his body isn't there. Her heart is broken; grief consumes her.

She is so distraught that although she actually sees Jesus, she mistakes him for the gardener. And even though Jesus literally speaks directly to her, she fails to recognize him.

Then, he says her name.

Instantly, she knows it's him. Instantly, she falls at his feet. Instantly, she clings to him.

He says her name.

There is deep intimacy and profound affection that emanates from this sacred address: Mary.

He says her name. She knows THAT voice. She knows the way HE says her name. She has heard it many times. It's a very personal moment. It's a deeply profound moment. It's a holy moment.

Sister, he knows your name too. With the same deep intimacy and profound affection, He whispers YOUR name. He has endured excruciating agony to make you his. He has been to hell and back for you. He longs that you would personally and intimately know His voice, that the sound of his voice would penetrate every corner of your soul. You mean that much to him!

Today, listen to his voice through his word. Learn his voice. Sit with him. Let the love in his voice permeate every facet of your being. Your name brings joy to his heart.

> *The sheep hear his voice, and he calls his own sheep by name and leads them out. When he has brought out all his own, he*

goes before them, and the sheep follow him, for they know his voice. (John 10:3–4)

Chapter Seventy-Nine
FULFILLING A PURPOSE

*The LORD will fulfill his purpose for me;
your steadfast love, O LORD, endures forever.
Do not forsake the work of your hands.*
Psalm 138:8

Saint Patrick was born in England (not Ireland) in the 5th century. As a teenager, he was kidnapped by Irish raiders and taken to Ireland as a slave. He spent six years in captivity laboring as a shepherd.

During that difficult and lonely season, he experienced a profound encounter with God and converted to Christianity. After escaping slavery, he returned home to England and studied for the priesthood. Following his ordination, he returned to Ireland as his mission field! He went back to the land of his bondage with a passion to see the pagan nation, where he had once been enslaved, set free. Amazing!

I doubt this is how Patrick would have written his own story. My guess is that he could have done without the kidnapping, the six years of homesickness, the bondage of being a slave, and the fear of what his future held. He probably would have preferred to stay on his family's wealthy estate and enjoy the safety and comforts of home.

But the Author of all stories had quite a different idea in mind (as he often does!). Though not without pain and trial, his design for the life of this one man was unbelievably glorious. His plan reached far beyond the wildest imagination of a young English boy.

Sister, the same is true for you. The Father was and is writing his magnificent Story of Redemption across the pages of history and ***you are a part of that wonderful Story.*** A valuable and unique part. God has a specific and personal plan for your life that HE WILL ACCOMPLISH by his grace. In fact, he is more committed to accomplishing his purpose than you are!

Wherever you are today, know that God is at work fulfilling his good purpose for your life. He is at work in your trials, in your triumphs, and even when it feels like your life is at a standstill.

Not one circumstance, relationship, or detail of your life is beyond the scope of his love, care, purpose, and design. Your Father has chosen you to be his and is therefore unwaveringly committed to you and to your part in his glorious story. Sometimes in our suffering and pain or even in our apathy, it's hard to believe that God is really at work for our good and his glory.

If that is where you find yourself today, confess that to him. He invites you to come to him with your doubts, confusion, and hurt. Where is he asking you to trust what he says over what you feel? In what circumstance do you find yourself doubting that he is present in the midst of it? Ask him for the grace to believe what you cannot see.

Chapter Eighty

I GOT ADOPTED! I GOT ADOPTED!

But when the fullness of time had come, God sent forth his Son, born of woman, born under the law, to redeem those who were under the law, so that we might receive adoption as sons. And because you are sons, God has sent the Spirit of his Son into our hearts, crying, "Abba, Father!" So you are no longer a slave, but a son, and if a son, then an heir through God.
Galatians 4:4–7

This past year, our cousins adopted two precious girls whom they fostered from infancy. The adoption process, though full of joy and laughter, was also grueling at times. Unkept visits with disinterested biological parents, flaws and inconsistencies in the social service system, judges who came and went (with each new judge the case practically started over), and the threat of losing the girls constantly weighed on their hearts and minds. Additionally, though the sisters were so

young, sadly, they knew of the possibility that they would one day be forced to leave the only place they ever knew as home.

When the adoption became official, the entire family was overjoyed! Parents, grandparents, cousins, aunts, uncles, neighbors, church members, friends—everyone who knows this family was ecstatic. The delight was uncontainable.

But no one was more relieved and delighted than these two sweet girls.

To celebrate, the family enjoyed a weeklong grand vacation in a child's paradise. From the moment of arrival until the day of departure, the girls donned celebratory buttons. Everywhere they went, they proudly wore those buttons. Whenever someone noticed their buttons and asked what they were celebrating, they each cheered and danced, "I Got Adopted! I Got Adopted!"

Adoption is everything for them. Forever, they are part of a family who loves them and will never leave them. Forever, they share their mom and dad's name. Forever, they belong. Forever they are safe. Forever, they are part of a new story.

You too are adopted, Sister. You are forever part of a family who loves you. Forever, you share the name of your Father—you have been sealed by His Spirit as a guarantee that you belong to him forever. Forever, you are safe. Forever, you are part of the most glorious Story ever written.

Your adoption brings joy and delight to God. He has loved you since before the foundation of the world. But, like my cousins, the process of your adoption was also grueling. The One who offered his perfect life for you suffered tortuously to secure your welcome into the family. His body, mind, and soul were afflicted to bring you home. Yet, his love was greater than the pain of his suffering. He fought for you. And he won.

So, celebrate. Dance! Cheer! Tell everyone who asks why you're so happy: "I Got Adopted!"

Chapter Eighty-One
WELL-PROVED

*God is our refuge and strength,
a very present help in trouble.*
Psalm 46:1

Several years ago, we replaced our front stone patio. After 50 years of snow, ice, shoveling, salt, and general wear and tear, our walkway completely disintegrated. The entry steps crumbled under your feet. Replacing the collapsed masonry was inevitable. However, before reconstruction began, we researched several hardscaping companies searching for a business with a well-proven track record of excellence and dependability.

Psalm 46 is a hymn recounting God's faithfulness, provision, protection, and the promise of his Presence. The song begins with a declaration that God is a very present help in trouble.

According to the ESV Study Bible footnote, the word "present," also translates as "well-proved.'" **Our God is well-proven.** Time and time again, he validated that he is who he says he is. He proved his faithfulness when he delivered Israel from the Egyptians. He demonstrated his provision when the people of God wandered in the wilderness for forty years. He confirmed his power when he repeatedly destroyed the enemies of his people.

But above all, he has definitively proven his love for us by sacrificing his one and only Son. Romans 5:8 says, *"But God shows his love for us in that while we were still sinners, Christ died for us."*

Even when we hated him, he loved us. Even when we ignored him, he loved us. And he manifested his perfect love by becoming a person and dying the death that you and I should have died.

When the circumstances of life look like God is not loving, remind yourself that he is well-proved. When the weight of painful relationships suggests that God is far away, remember that he came near. He already demonstrated that he can be trusted. He proved his extravagant love for you by dying for you.

What's more, Paul tells us, *"He who did not spare his own Son but gave him up for us all, how will he not also with him graciously give us all things?"* (Romans 8:32). He will never fail to prove himself faithful. This is who he always has been, who he is, and who he always will be.

Are you struggling to trust God today? Is it hard for you to believe that he is your refuge and strength? Are you desperate for help today? Instead of focusing on your circumstances or even your lack of faith, remember that your God is well-proven.

He can be trusted. He has demonstrated his love, his faithfulness, his goodness, and his power in the person and work of his Son, Jesus.

Center your attention on him today. Let the reality of his proven track record buttress your trust in him.

Chapter Eighty-Two
SURGERY

Purge me with hyssop, and I shall be clean; wash me, and I shall be whiter than snow. Let me hear joy and gladness; let the bones that you have broken rejoice. Hide your face from my sins, and blot out all my iniquities.
Psalm 51:7–9

After months of pain and immobility and weeks of physical therapy, my youngest son underwent surgery. A torn labrum and a hip impingement necessitated operative repair.

His condition required that the doctor cut him open and remove the part of his bone that was both causing further damage to his body and inflicting consistent suffering.

Surgery was a gift. Was it painful? Absolutely. Has the healing been slow? For sure. Has recovery at times brought more pain?

Definitely. Has he been forced to rely on others for help far more than he wants? 100 percent!

But, the surgery was a gift. Without the tearing, scraping, and agony of the surgical repair, there was no hope for total healing. No hope of pain-free running. No hope of playing basketball again.

The surgery crushed him. He was helpless afterward. He was in pain. He was physically, mentally, and emotionally worn down. But he was on the road to healing.

Psalm 51 was written by King David in the aftermath of his greatest sin. David committed adultery with another man's wife and then had this man killed in hopes of covering up his own iniquity. It's a low point in his life for sure.

Thankfully, God sends his good friend Nathan who calls him out on his sin (we all need friends like Nathan!). As he confesses his sin to the Lord, he acknowledges that his sin has crushed him. That's what sin does—it kills us. It steals the life right out of us. And if left unconfessed, it destroys. Listen to what David says in Psalm 32:3–4 about his sin:

For when I kept silent, my bones wasted away through my groaning all day long. For day and night, your hand was heavy upon me; my strength was dried up as by the heat of summer.

Unconfessed sin saps the life out of us. It is an unbearable weight that slowly kills everything in its wake. Confession breaks the power. Like the surgery, is it painful? Absolutely! Is the healing process following repentance slow? For sure. When sin is confessed, are there consequences to address that crush us? Definitely. Do we need to rely on others to help us war against our flesh? 100 percent!

But, confessing sin is a gift. Without the admittance of, repentance of, and confession of sin, there is no hope of healing. No hope for freedom. No hope for lasting joy. With an acknowledgment and sorrow for sin, the healing power of the Gospel is unleashed in our lives. Freedom, joy, and growth follow.

Where are you today? Is the weight of sin crushing you? Do you need the courage to confess your sin to a trusted friend? Your Savior stands by ready and eager to forgive. Do not wait another day. Let today be your day of freedom!

Chapter Eighty-Three
TRUST THE PROCESS

And he said, "The Kingdom of God is as if a man should scatter seed on the ground. He sleeps and rises night and day, and the seed sprouts and grows; he knows not how. The earth produces by itself, first the blade, then the ear, then the full grain in the ear. But when the grain is ripe, at once he puts in the sickle, because the harvest has come."
Mark 4:26–29

Trust the process.

We hear this phrase when rehabilitating from an injury or surgery.

Trust the process.

We hear it when starting a new exercise routine.

Trust the process.

We hear it when learning to play an instrument.

Trust the process.

We hear it when potty training.

Trust the process. The phrase is meant to inspire hope.

Trust the process when taking small steps towards a goal while the results are not immediately visible.

The Kingdom of God is a work of process as well. It's a process that God begins, and he promises to complete (Philippians 1:6). It's a process in which he is actively and purposefully at work in us. And in the midst of it, he invites us to trust him.

How does the process of Kingdom growth work? Mark 4 teaches us.

Often when God is at work, the *process is slow.* **Growth takes time**. First, the seed is scattered, and then days and nights (and more days and nights) pass before the seed sprouts. After the seed bursts through the ground, the blade begins to develop. And it grows SLOWLY.

Days and nights pass (and more days and nights) and still only a blade remains. One day the ear develops. Then, more days and more nights. Finally, the full grain is on the ear. It is a long process; time passes slowly. Throughout the process, it is tempting to wonder, "Will this seed ever bear fruit?" But, we remember that God is always at work in us—even when we "see" no sprout yet.

Second, **God's ways are not our ways**. As the growth comes, the Scripture tells us that the man *"he knows not how."*

Sometimes we want to know exactly how God is going to work in our current circumstances, when he is going to bring some kind of change and through whom he is going to act. But, we don't always get to know that. God's ways are not our ways—*"...the seed sprouts and grows; he knows not how."*

Third, we observe that **fruit will come.** God will produce fruit because he promised he would produce in us that which is pleasing to him. Even though it may seem slow to us and even though we don't understand his ways, we remind ourselves that God is always at work, and he brings growth!

> *And I am sure of this, that he who began a good work in you will bring it to completion at the day of Jesus Christ.*
> (Philippians 1:6)

Chapter Eighty-Four
A GLIMPSE INSIDE

> *Jesus, knowing that the Father had given all things into his hands, and that he had come from God, and was going back to God, rose from supper.*
> John 13:3–4a

Astronomy has always fascinated me. I remember being in elementary school when the mobile planetarium visited our class. On the floor in the dark, we gazed up at the brilliant night sky full of stars trying to identify different constellations and distant planets.

Still today, I wake up at 3:00 a.m., wrap up in lots of blankets, and venture outside to watch a winter meteor shower or catch a glimpse of a solar phenomenon. While all of these wonders always exist in our galaxy, there are only special seasons when we actually get a glimpse of the magnificent.

In John 13, the heart and mind of the Magnificent One can

be glimpsed. It is a rare treasure when the Holy Spirit allows us to peek into the thoughts of our Savior. Jesus and his disciples are gathered for their last meal together before our Messiah goes to the cross.

John tells us that Jesus knows, *"...his hour has come to depart from this world...."* Let's not pass too quickly over this phrase. Jesus is about to be betrayed by a dear friend, abandoned by all his followers, suffer under the hands of ruthless enemies, die a death he doesn't deserve, and be forsaken by his Father. This is a grave moment of deep and isolating sorrow.

And yet, despite his own imminent suffering, the heart of Jesus is to move towards, and not away from his disciples. He prepares to serve them by humbling himself to the place of the lowest servant and washing their feet.

> *Jesus, knowing that the Father had given all things into his hands, and that he had come from God and was going back to God, rose from supper... poured water into a basin and began to wash the disciples' feet....* (John 13:3–5)

Here is where we catch a beautiful glimpse into the heart and mind of our Suffering Servant.

The Spirit shows us his thoughts, *"Jesus, knowing that the Father had given all things into his hands...."* In that moment, Jesus remembers God's sovereignty. In light of his impending suffering and sorrow, God's control over every detail and facet of creation was at the forefront of His mind.

What a reminder for us! Wherever you are today, whether in the midst of broken relationships, deep grief, overwhelming anxiety, or an apathy that seems paralyzing, remember God is perfectly sovereign. There is not one tiny detail of your life over which God is not ruling. Every single day of your life has been written in his book before even one of them came to be (Psalm 139:16). Like Jesus, it is good for us to remember our God is the uncontested King.

Remember who he is.

Going further, in this intense moment of looming despair, Jesus considers his identity: *"Jesus, knowing that the Father had given all things into his hands, and that he had come from God...."* In these minutes, with his crucifixion coming within 24 hours, Jesus' thoughts focus on the fact that he has come from God. He remembers the One to whom he belongs and this reality is a source of comfort and strength for him. The same holds true for us. Identity changes everything; who you are in Christ is your truest reality. You belong to the One who has determined, before the foundation of the world was laid, to set his love and affection on you and to make you his.

Remember who you are.

Finally, we see that Jesus looks to the future.

Jesus, knowing that the Father had given all things into his hands, and that he had come from God and was going back to God, rose from supper. (John 13:3–4a)

For him, the present moment wasn't all that there was. The fact that a better day was coming anchored his mind as the most horrendous and glorious moment in history approached.

One day, there will be no more suffering, no more sorrow, and no more pain. Every wrong will be made right. Wherever you are today, this is your hope too. A better day is guaranteed.

Remember your future. The Magnificent has made himself known. He has chosen to reveal his loving and gracious heart to the ones he has claimed for his delight. May the truth of who he is, who you are, and the reality of your glorious future, strengthen your heart and mind as you trust him today.

Chapter Eighty-Five

BREAD TRUCKS AND BENEFITS

*Blessed be the God and Father of our
Lord Jesus Christ, who has blessed us in Christ
with every spiritual blessing in the heavenly places.*
Ephesians 1:3

One recent January, traffic on I-95 came to a standstill due to snow and ice. Passengers were stuck in their cars for almost 24 hours without food, water, heat, or bathrooms!

A story of generosity and hope spread across the internet. One woman noticed a food truck among the stranded vehicles. Inspired, she contacted the company to ask if the food on the truck could be shared with her very cold, tired, and hungry fellow travelers.

Within moments, the CEO of the company responded, and the driver of the truck immediately distributed bread to the stranded drivers. He was instantly a hero, and his picture flooded the news. The driver was celebrated and praised for his kindness.

As I listened to the heartwarming story of brotherly love, I was struck by the fact that the driver of the truck reaped all the benefits (praise, joy, recognition) of the owner's generosity. On the other hand, the owner bore all the cost.

While it probably also brought the owner joy to donate bread to the weary travelers, his gift was not without sacrifice.

Furthermore, it was the young woman who initiated the giving. She phoned the bread company and began the process of rescue. Yet again, the driver received the benefit. By someone else's design and at someone else's willingness to bear the cost, he experienced delight and adoration.

Doesn't this remind you a little of our story too? Even though we didn't initiate a relationship with God, we reap the benefits of his pursuit (Ephesians 1:3–5). As a beneficiary, we receive every spiritual blessing in the heavenly places including adoption, holiness, love!

Second, although we could never pay the cost of our sins, we are clothed with the benefits of his sacrifice (2 Corinthians 5:21). His righteousness is ours!

Finally, though we certainly do not deserve any glory for what our Savior accomplished, we are transformed from glory to glory (2 Corinthians 3:18). What a generous God we have!

I can only imagine the joy the truck driver experienced as he ventured from vehicle to vehicle bringing the gift of free bread to starving, stranded, cold travelers. It was not his idea to give out free bread, nor did it cost him a thing. Yet, he was blessed. May the initiating love of the Father and the cost of the Son's sacrifice remind your heart that you are loved and blessed. In him, you receive every spiritual blessing. Let your heart feast on your blessings today!

Chapter Eighty-Six
THE FENCE

What then shall we say? That the law is sin? By no means! Yet if it had not been for the law, I would not have known sin. For I would not have known what it is to covet if the law had not said, "You shall not covet." But sin, seizing an opportunity through the commandment, produced in me all kinds of covetousness. For apart from the law, sin lies dead.
Romans 7:7–8

A mile of electric fence surrounds our pastures. Touching the charged wire discharges a harrowing shock wave through your fingers, up your arm, through your elbow, and all the way to your shoulder. An unpleasant jolt with lingering discomfort.

Whenever anyone visits the farm, we caution, *"Don't touch the electric fence."* And you guessed it—inevitably and immediately, they desperately want to touch the fence. No one who ever touches the fence says, "Oh, that wasn't that bad." It's always worse than they imagined.

This is how sin works. It seizes every opportunity to produce evil inside of us. As soon as we're commanded, "Don't do that," this is the very thing we earnestly desire to do. Then, after having succumbed to the temptation, the guilt and consequence brings pain and shame. Paul argues this exact point, exclaiming, *"For I do not understand my own actions. For I do not do what I want, but I do the very thing I hate"* (Romans 7:15).

Paul is not alone in his dilemma, right? You have undoubtedly wrestled in that tension too. In your heart, you love God's law and desire to please the Lord, but evil always lies close at hand. What I want to do, I don't do. What I don't want to do, this I keep on doing!

At the end of his inner conflict, exasperated, Paul concedes, *"Wretched man that I am! Who will deliver me from this body of death?"* (Romans 7:24).

I love this! There is hope here! Amidst the sin war that will forever rage this side of eternity, he throws up his arms in surrender. He casts himself on the mercy of God. He reminds his soul, *"Thanks be to God through Jesus Christ our Lord!"* (Romans 7:25)

And one verse later, *"There is therefore now no condemnation for those who are in Christ Jesus"* (Romans 8:1).

In the fight against sin, Paul arms himself with surrender. He falls on the mercy of God. He doesn't look inside his own heart for more strength or greater willpower.

Instead, **he banks his hope for transformation on the grace of God.** Sister, as you battle the sin that plagues your heart, remember freedom is birthed from surrender. Plunge yourself into the mercy of God. His grace never fails. For those who belong to him, he has no wrath left—he poured it all out on his perfect Son. So, don't despair in your battle with sin. But, run to Jesus, who loves to forgive you more than you long to be forgiven. Run to the One who longs to pour out his Spirit and free you from slavery even more than you desire to be free.

What good news for struggling sinners like you and me!

Chapter Eighty-Seven
REMEMBER & RETELL

And David said, "The LORD who delivered me from the paw of the lion and from the paw of the bear will deliver me from the hand of this Philistine." And Saul said to David, "Go, and the LORD be with you."
1 Samuel 17:37

In this familiar account of David and Goliath, we eavesdrop on a conversation between a shepherd boy and King Saul. Israel is at war with their Philistine enemy. Everyone in the Hebrew camp cowers in fear.

But David, who arrived merely to deliver supplies, volunteers to battle the giant Goliath. Sizing up the young boy, King Saul vocalizes  his doubts. Yet instead of flinching under the king's lack of confidence, David recalls God's past faithfulness. He remembers when he fought the lion and the bear. He recalls God's power and deliverance. And **he banks his future victory on the Lord's past salvation.**

Remembering and retelling is a theme throughout the Scriptures. God continually exhorts his people to remember what he had accomplished for them and retell it over and over again.

> *When your children ask in time to come, "What do these stones mean to you?" Then you shall tell them that the waters of the Jordan were cut off before the ark of the covenant of the LORD. When it passed over the Jordan, the waters of the Jordan were cut off. So these stones shall be to the people of Israel a memorial forever.* (Joshua 4:6–7)

> *Here my cry, O God, listen to my prayer; from the end of the earth I call to you when my heart is faint… for you have been my refuge, a strong tower against the enemy.* (Psalm 61:1–3)

> *I will remember the deeds of the LORD; yes, I will remember your wonders of old.* (Psalm 77:11)

> *And he took bread, and when he had given thanks, he broke it and gave it to them saying, "This is my body, which is given for you. Do this in remembrance of me."* (Luke 22:19)

The same exhortation exists for us. Remember and retell.

Remember what God has done and talk about it over and over again, with everyone who will listen. Not only does it bring glory to God but the retelling bolsters our faith. We remind our hearts of the faithfulness and goodness of God. In the same way that David's confidence in defeating Goliath rested on God's past dependability, so too **God's faithfulness to us anchors our present strength.**

So today, remember. Take some time to recall specific, personal ways that God has demonstrated his faithfulness to you. Make a list. Write it down. Rehearse it in your mind. Call your friend and tell her about it before going to sleep. Remember and retell.

Chapter Eighty-Eight
DOGS

For his invisible attributes, namely, his eternal power and divine nature, have been clearly perceived, ever since the creation of the world, in the things that have been made. So they are without excuse.
Romans 1:20

He is the image of the invisible God, the firstborn of all creation. For by him all things were created, in heaven and on earth, visible and invisible, whether thrones or dominions or rulers or authorities—all things were created through him and for him.
Colossians 1:15–16

I adore my two black labs; they are the sweetest of companions. Whenever I walk through the door, without fail, with their tails furiously wagging, they joyously bound to the door, welcoming me home as if they've waited all day for this moment. When my heart is heavy with the cares of this world, they remain close to my heels - their soft fur brushing against my shins, reminding me with their presence that I am not alone. When I'm irritable, and through no fault of their own become the target of my impatience, they repeatedly and immediately forgive. Almost instantaneously they re-engage, absolving their ranting owner with kisses.

The intended purpose of everything in creation is the glory of God. The Scriptures teach us that Jesus is the centerpiece of all eternity and that all things were created by him and through him and *for him.*

I've hesitated to write about how a dog's disposition points us to the faithfulness and tenderness of God for fear that in some way the glory of God might be diminished in such a weak illustration. Yet, if creation is intended to direct us to the One who is deserving of all praise and adoration, then such a connection seems permissible.

If God's invisible attributes are revealed by what has been made, then it seems fair game to compare (even if the likening is insufficient) the affection of the Father with a dog's adoration.

In a similar, but far grander way, the Father delights in the presence of his children. You are a joy to his heart. You are always welcome in his presence. Never will he cast you away.

> *The Lord your God is in your midst, a mighty one who will save; he will rejoice over you with gladness; he will quiet you by his love; he will exult over you with loud singing.* (Zephaniah 3:17)

In a similar, but far more glorious way, when your heart is heavy, when the sorrows of this life blanket every waking moment, your Father remains close. In his perfect compassion, he actually draws near to our aching souls: *"The LORD is close to the brokenhearted and saves the crushed in spirit"* (Psalm 34:18).

And in a similar, but far more magnificent way, your Father is quick to forgive you because of the astonishing and atoning sacrifice of his Son. The perfect righteousness of Christ is yours because you belong to Jesus.

> *For as high as the heavens are above the earth, so great is his steadfast love toward those who fear him; as far as the east is from the west, so far does he remove our transgressions from us. As a father shows compassion to his children so the Lord shows compassion to those who fear him.* (Psalm 103:11–13)

So today, as you observe the glories of creation, pause. Let what has been made by our wonderful Creator remind you of the invisible attributes of the One who welcomes you into his presence, rejoices over you with loud singing, never leaves your side, and forgives all your sins. He is worthy of all our praise!

Chapter Eighty-Nine
UNITY

Therefore, if you are offering your gift at the altar and there remember that your brother or sister has something against you, leave your gift there in front of the altar. First go and be reconciled to them; then come and offer your gift.
Matthew 5:23–24

A group of women from my church are reading through the Bible together this year. To be on this journey with other sisters is incredibly encouraging. We support and cheer one another on as we travel through the Scriptures  (and we all need a little extra motivation when we're reading certain books!).

As one, we follow the same plan and read the same Scriptures each day. Most of the time, there are several chapters per day. On average, reading requires about 15–20 minutes a day.

That being said, recently, there was an unusual shift in the plan. Unlike any other day, there was only one psalm, and it was a really short one, Psalm 133:

Behold, how good and pleasant it is
when brothers dwell in unity!
It is like the precious oil on the head,
running down on the beard,
on the beard of Aaron,
running down on the collar of his robes!
It is like the dew of Hermon,
which falls on the mountains of Zion!
For there the Lord has commanded the blessing,
life forevermore.

I have no idea why the creators of this chronological reading plan decided to appoint only one psalm for this day. But to me, the appointment screams of the heart of God. His deep desire (as evidenced in Jesus' high priestly prayer) is for his people to live together in unity for in that place of unity, he commands his blessing.

In fact, we see this imperative over and over again in Scripture:

- Love one another
- Forgive one another
- Bear one another's burdens
- Be patient with one another
- Keep no record of wrongs
- Lay down your life for others
- By your love for each other, the world will know that you are my disciples

Living in unity with people is far from easy. Getting along with family, friends, or even church members proves very challenging. We are selfish people living with other selfish people.

Yet, as Christ-Followers, we are called to more. Christianity is radical. To follow hard after Jesus isn't easy—no one ever said it would be. Offering forgiveness is costly for sure. Letting insults go requires incredible strength.

But, it's worth it.

So where are you today? Do you have an unresolved conflict with a friend? Are you harboring bitterness in your heart towards a brother or sister? Have you withheld forgiveness because you were wronged? Do you avoid ***her*** at all costs?

Sister, you are called to more. You belong to Jesus. And he commands his blessing in the unity of his people. So, go. Go and be reconciled. Go and find freedom. Go and enjoy the blessing of God.

Chapter Ninety
FIREFIGHTERS

For he has rescued us from the dominion of darkness and brought us into the kingdom of the Son he loves, in whom we have redemption, the forgiveness of sins.
Colossians 1:13–14

During my junior year of college, a fellow student of mine was a volunteer firefighter. The instantaneous way he responded when the siren blared always brought me to the verge of tears. As soon as that alarm sounded, he gathered his notebooks, packed up his textbooks, and furiously darted out the door. He was laser-focused. In those few seconds, everyone in that room stopped, held their breath, watched, and waited.

At that moment, rescue trumped everything. At that moment, nothing stopped him from bolting out the door, flying down the steps, and sprinting across campus to the firehouse. At that moment, he put his own life in danger to save someone else's. At that moment, we were all grateful for rescuers.

Sister, you too have a Rescuer.

You have a Rescuer who not only risked his life to save yours but sacrificed himself to ransom you from the dominion of darkness. Your rescue trumped the pain, suffering, betrayal, and death that Jesus endured.

In fact, the Scriptures tell us that it was for the joy set before him that Jesus suffered on the cross. For the joy of saving you! Nothing could stop him from stepping down from his glorious place in heaven to rescue you from the grip that sin held on your life. Nothing!

What's more—not only did he rescue you from the kingdom of darkness but he has brought you into a new kingdom. A kingdom of forgiveness, freedom, power, and joy. A kingdom of belonging and hope. A kingdom of that will never end.

Here's the absolutely mind-blowing truth in all this—it was his delight in and love for you that drove him to rescue. Sister, never ever forget how deeply you are loved and the price that your Rescuer paid for your soul.

Remember, you belong to a different kingdom now. You are a permanent citizen of a heavenly kingdom.

So go and be who you are today. Live in the light of your new identity. Don't return to your former kingdom; you don't belong there anymore. Instead, *let your light so shine before men that they see your good works and glorify your Father in heaven* (Matthew 5:16).

> *Fixing our eyes on Jesus, the pioneer and perfecter of faith.*
> *For the joy set before him he endured the cross, scorning its*
> *shame, and sat down at the right hand of the throne of God.*
> (Hebrews 12:2)

Chapter Ninety-One
STUBBED TOES

For you formed my inward parts; you knitted me together in my mother's womb. I praise you, for I am fearfully and wonderfully made. Wonderful are your works; my soul knows it very well.
Psalm 139:13–14

The other morning I stubbed my big toe really badly on the threshold of the bathroom floor. Man, did it hurt! Instantly, I examined my foot, expecting it to be covered in blood, deeply bruised, or ripped open.

Of course, it wasn't. Rarely does a "stub" draw blood. But still, surely with such intense pain, there should be some kind of evidence of injury.

As simple as this sounds, my dramatic little mishap caused me to consider the complexity and magnificence of the human body. Now, it is true that nothing at all was, or is, wrong with my toe. I am perfectly fine.

But, IF something was wrong, my body would've alerted me

with pain. The fact that God created our bodies to respond to harm with pain amazes me.

Imagine if we hurt ourselves and the body did NOT respond with pain. Imagine how long a wound would go untreated if we didn't have the pain cue to alert us that our body needed attention and care.

This is not rocket science, but I love how God takes the simple (and sometimes irritating—because I was really irritated when I stubbed my toe!) things of life and teaches us about how amazing he is.

A sunset reveals his beauty. A vibrantly colored tropical fish reveals his creativity. A near miss of an accident reveals his protection. A delicious meal reveals his love for enjoyment. A friend's call reveals his compassion.

Our God is spectacular. As you enjoy this new day, remember that he is marvelous in his creative power; and you, Sister, are fearfully and wonderfully made. Creation shouts of his magnificence! As part of the wonder of his handiwork, you are called to be a herald of his glory too. Today, join with the heavens in praising the Lord!

> *Praise the Lord! Praise the Lord from the heavens; praise him in the heights! Praise him, all his angels; praise him, all his hosts! Praise him, sun and moon, praise him, all you shining stars Praise him, you highest heavens, and you waters above the heavens! Let them praise the name of the Lord! For he commanded and they were created.* (Psalm 148:1–5)

Chapter Ninety-Two
SECRET THINGS

*The secret things belong to the Lord our God, but
the things that are revealed belong to us and to our
children forever, that we may do all the words of this law.*
Deuteronomy 29:29

A few years ago, my mom was diagnosed with breast cancer. I remember the two of us sitting across from the doctor as she explained this particular type of cancer. In great detail and with articulate diagrams, she described how the cells mutate and how the tissues change as the cancer grows 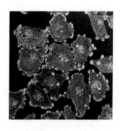 and spreads. She implored medical words that were foreign to us, and we followed her scientific analysis for about thirty seconds. At the end of the visit, it all came down to one question: *Do we trust her?*

Life is full of uncertainty. What will tomorrow hold? Will there be reconciliation in my relationships? How will this health crisis turn out? What if I lose my job? The future abounds with uncertainty. In the midst of all the unknown, it all comes down to one question: *In what do I place my trust?*

This passage from Deuteronomy brings comfort to my heart in the midst of a life full of uncertainty. From this verse, there are three truths upon which we anchor our trust. First of all, we observe that there are secret things, things that we will never know and aren't meant to know. God's ways are not our ways; his thoughts are not our thoughts. He sees and understands the world in a way that is beyond our comprehension. Yet, although we can't know God exhaustively, we can know him truly. He has revealed himself in his Word and so with assurance, we affirm that he is always good, that he is always loving and he is always sovereign. So, in all the unknowing of life, will you trust the One who knows?

Second, immediately after God tells us that there are things in this life that we will not know or understand, he reminds us of who he is" *"The secret things belong to **the Lord our God.**"* He is a personal God who designed us to enjoy an intimate relationship with him. Just a few verses before, the Lord says this, *"For you are a people holy to the Lord your God. The Lord your God has chosen you to be a people for his treasured possession"* (Deuteronomy 7:6).

Sometimes we can associate secrecy with distance. Or if someone keeps a secret from us, we assume they are being dishonest or unloving. But God reminds us that while there are secret things, he is a personal, loving God who dearly treasures us. So, in the unknowing of life, will you trust the One who is for you?

The third point we observe is that ***everything that you need to know, he has revealed to you.*** To live the life of obedience to which you were called and to flourish as a child of God who enjoys and glorifies God, you know everything you need to know. So with all that he provides, will you trust him?

Today, in the midst of all the uncertainty that surrounds you, will you trust him? Will you trust the One who knows it all? Will you put your hope in the One who loves you more than you could ever imagine? Will you trust the One who has revealed and given to you all that you need to run the race he sets before you?

Sister, he is worthy of your trust.

Chapter Ninety-Three
5 MORE POUNDS

Now for a little while you may have had to suffer grief in all kinds of trials. These have come so that your faith— of greater worth than gold, which perishes even though refined by fire—may be proved genuine and may result in praise, glory and honor when Jesus Christ is revealed.
1 Peter 1:6–7 (NIV)

At our gym, we are constantly pushed to work harder and lift more than we think we can. My coach often approaches me with a weight that is about 5 pounds heavier than the one I am lifting.

My response is always the same: I can't lift that much. Then his response is the same: I bet you can.

The scene frequently repeats. I whine and complain while he stands and waits patiently, unwavering in his decision.

Eventually, I attempt it. I struggle. I wince. I barely lift it.

But usually, he's right. I can do it. It isn't easy. It isn't comfortable. It isn't without pain. But, he knew I could do it. I was the one who didn't believe I could.

When he is pushing me beyond what I think I can do, he isn't trying to prove to himself that I am stronger than I think. He wants to prove it to me. He wants to convince me that my goals are too small and my confidence is too weak.

In this epistle, the apostle Peter encourages persecuted and suffering Christians to remain faithful as they endure adversity and hardship. Without diminishing the severity of their trials, he reminds them of God's power and sovereignty. These trials, he exhorts, serve to prove that their faith is genuine! What? Trials prove what? They prove that faith is genuine. To whom? To whom is this faith being proven genuine?

Certainly, not to God. He already knows everything.

Amazingly, it is for our sake! God wants to prove to us that our faith is real. Our endurance in and perseverance through the hardships of life are employed by God to demonstrate **to us** that our faith is genuine.

You see, just like my coach knows that I can do more than I think I can, the Father knows that your faith is real. Do you know how he is so sure of that? Because your faith is a gift from him! He is absolutely certain that your faith will be proved genuine because he is the Author, Perfecter, and Sustainer of it! And in his exorbitant kindness, he desires for you to be secure in the certainty of your faith too. Isn't that amazing?

When the trials of life overwhelm you, when you feel like your faith is shaken, in your weakest moments, remember that he is at work. Faith is a gift. He will hold you firm to the end.

And on that glorious day when Jesus Christ is revealed, your very real faith will result in praise, glory, and honor! What great news!

Chapter Ninety-Four
FINISH LINES

Not that I have already obtained this or am already perfect, but I press on to make it my own, because Christ Jesus has made me his own. Brothers, I do not consider that I have made it my own. But one thing I do: forgetting what lies behind and straining forward to what lies ahead, I press on toward the goal for the prize of the upward call of God in Christ Jesus.
Philippians 3:12–14

In 1996, a dear friend of mine raced in the Philadelphia marathon. His girlfriend and I accompanied him to the race in order to cheer and encourage him along the way. At various points along the route, spectators gather to spur their runners on.

Marathons are grueling. When he finally crossed the finish line, he nearly fainted. Immediately we wrapped him in a foil blanket and ushered him over to the museum steps. Drained and exhausted, he collapsed to his knees.

But then something wildly extraordinary happened. Reaching into his sock, he withdrew a small pocket knife. Slowly, he lifted the knife to his collar, reached under his turtleneck, and cut the twine necklace from his neck. A diamond ring slid off the string. Right there, in the middle of chaos and crowd, shaking with exhaustion and joy, he proposed.

After she said yes, and we recovered from the shock of this incredible moment, he told us that this proposal was the reason he completed the race. He knew what was coming at the end. His eyes were fixed on his future bride. He absolutely MUST cross that finish line.

The prize at the end was the motivation to continue. The reward was inspiring. The future compelled the present.

Paul teaches us the same thing. He urges us to look forward, to fix our eyes on what lies ahead, to set our minds on the prize of eternity. His encouragement to endure the present is to laser our focus on the future.

Today, remind yourself of what lies ahead. A marvelous future awaits you. Your inheritance is guaranteed. The One who delights to call you his beloved will one day welcome you home. You will see him face to face. He will smile at you. You will see your faith with your eyes.

There will be no more sadness, no more fear, no more loneliness, no more pain. There will be only beauty and joy and laughter and glory. Let the reality of what is yet to come anchor today's hope.

Chapter Ninety-Five
ONE FOR THE MANY

*Because of this the king was angry and very furious, and
commanded that all the wise men of Babylon be destroyed.
So the decree went out, and the wise men were about to be killed;
and they sought Daniel and his companions, to kill them.*
Daniel 2:12–13

*Therefore Daniel went in to Arioch, whom the king had appointed
to destroy the wise men of Babylon. He went and said thus to him:
"Do not destroy the wise men of Babylon; bring me in
before the king, and I will show the king the interpretation."*
Daniel 2:24

While the people of Israel were living in exile in Babylon, King Nebuchadnezzar had a dream. Deeply troubled and desperate to ascertain its meaning, he called on the wise men, magicians, and enchanters of the land to both reveal and interpret his nighttime vision. Doomed to defeat by such an impossible demand, the interpreters failed. Nebuchadnezzar was furious and consequently sentenced all the wise men of the land to death.

Upon hearing of the king's order, Daniel requests an audience with the monarch. After calling on his trusted friends to pray, the Lord revealed both the contents of the dream and its interpretation to Daniel, who in turn divulged the mystery to his master. In response, Daniel was exalted by the king, and the wise men were spared.

What was set before the wise men of Babylon was an impossible task. They were utterly powerless to fulfill the demand of the king.

But then Daniel stepped in. Daniel, by God's miraculous intervention, succeeded where the diviners failed and as a result, the interpreters were saved. The Sovereign God rescued the many through the act of one man.

Imagine how relieved and overjoyed the wise men must have been when Daniel met the king's mandate! I wonder how they responded. Did they celebrate Daniel? Did they thank him? Did they stand in awe?

Many were rescued through the act of one man. This is our story too.

For as by the one man's disobedience the many were made sinners, so by the one man's obedience the many will be made righteous.
(Romans 5:19)

By his single act of sacrifice, Jesus has made us righteous before God! Like the wise men of Daniel's day, we were powerless to free ourselves from the just punishment due us. But the One saved the many. By His grace, there is now no condemnation for those who are in Christ (Romans 8:1).

What is our response to such good news? Do we celebrate Jesus? Do we thank him? Do we stand in awe? Paul, after declaring such a wonderful reality, encourages our response.

*We were buried therefore with him by baptism into death, in order that, just as Christ was raised from the dead by the glory of the Father, we too might **walk in newness of life.*** (Romans 6:4)

Sister, you are a new person. You are righteous before the living God! Your past no longer has the right to paralyze you. You have been rescued from death. Therefore, walk in newness of life. Be free!

Chapter Ninety-Six
KINTSUGI

> *But he said to me, "My grace is sufficient for you, for my power is made perfect in weakness." Therefore I will boast all the more gladly of my weaknesses, so that the power of Christ may rest upon me.*
> 2 Corinthians 12:9

Kintsugi is a Japanese art form in which broken objects (bowls, vases, plates) are mended back together with an adhesive that is overlaid with gold. The story of its inception goes like this:

A Japanese shogun broke his favorite tea bowl and sent it out for repair. When the refurbished piece was returned, the owner was grossly disappointed with the restoration and intended to discard the once-beloved piece. One of his craftsmen, upon hearing of the shogun's plan, repaired the bowl. But, instead of attempting to hide the flaws and imperfections, he highlighted them with precious metal. In the end, the tea bowl was more beautiful than its original perfection.

We've talked about the importance of stories—how we all have stories, stories that are meant to be shared, stories that are scarred by pain, betrayal, disappointment, sin, and brokenness. Sometimes, we desperately try to hide these fractures and cracks in our stories. But what if those flaws, imperfections, and broken parts are the very slits through which the grace of God is magnified?

What if, instead of trying to shroud those fractures, we highlight them? Even boast about them? What if it is through these imperfections that the grace, wonder, and beauty of God is most glorified?

Our Father is in the business of bringing beauty from brokenness. The crucifixion of Jesus is proof that from the most horrific events God shines his magnificence. In his sovereign grace and mercy, the darkest moment in human history serves as the glorious cornerstone of our faith.

So, we believe. We hope, against all hope, that he will bring beauty from the ashes. And when he does, we testify to it. We boast in our weakness that his power might be displayed.

As you wrestle with your shortcomings and failings, remember that God is always at work. The greatness of God in the face of your weakness is one of the tools God uses to strengthen the faith of his people. Rather than despise where you are, run to the One who delights in our dependence on him.

Today, as he gives you an opportunity, brag about him. Brag about your cracks. Let the rich beauty of the grace-covered fractures, like the gold-covered fractures on the Kintsugi bowl, bring glory to the God who loves to restore broken children.

Chapter Ninety-Seven

A LIFETIME OF UNLEARNING

> *For I am sure that neither death nor life, nor angels
> nor rulers, nor things present nor things to come, nor powers,
> nor height nor depth, nor anything else in all creation, will be
> able to separate us from the love of God in Christ Jesus our Lord.*
> Romans 8:38–39

In the seventh grade, a piece of paper slid onto my desk titled, "I Hate Judie Club." Below the crushing headline, dozens of classmates signed their names.

Needless to say, I was devastated and distraught. In a single moment, my entire world crumbled. I had absolutely no idea why everyone suddenly hated me, but they did.

I still cringe when I think about that day. I feel humiliation, shame, and ugliness. Out of that foundational experience came two deep-rooted beliefs that I will spend the rest of my life unlearning.

The first—there is something about who I am that is utterly

unlovable. The second—there is something about who I am that is entirely leavable.

Since that day, I spent my entire life striving to be someone who is worthy to be loved and worthy to be kept. This drive manifested itself predominantly with incessant pressure for perfection. Though from a young age I heard of God's love for me, damaging words dig deep roots.

Perhaps powerful lies entangle the roots of your faith too. Perhaps you also are relearning truths about who God is and who you are. It's not easy to unlearn a lie that has been reinforced in your heart over months, years or decades. Maybe you're weary, hopeless, or overwhelmed. I understand that—I've been there too.

That's why I love Jesus so much. He never grows weary in our unlearning. He reminds us that we are lovable and that he will never leave. He is never tempted to give up on you or to throw up his nail-pierced hands in frustration. He is not the least bit overwhelmed by you, frustrated by you, or exhausted by you. Rather, he whispers to your weary soul:

Come to me when you are weary and heavy laden and I will give you rest (Matthew 11:28).

Come to me for I am merciful and gracious, slow to anger and abounding in steadfast love (Psalm 103:8).

Come to me for I am patient and kind; I am not irritated by you nor do I resent you; I will endure this with you (1 Corinthians 13:4-7).

Come to me for I am transforming you from one degree of glory to another (2 Corinthians 3:18).

Come to me for I am making all things new (Revelation 21:5).

Sister, wherever you are today, whatever you are trying to unlearn about yourself or about him, whatever plagues your soul this day, remember—you are not alone.

Jesus will never leave you. You are lovable. He will never tire of you. He will never forsake you. He will transform you by his love. Rest in his promise.

Chapter Ninety-Eight
I NEED A LITTLE CHRISTMAS

In him was life, and the life was the light of men. The light shines in the darkness, and the darkness has not overcome it.
John 1:4–5

Every year it feels like Christmas comes a little earlier. Decorations are hung in October, Christmas music plays on the radio before Thanksgiving. Candy cane cocoa replaces "pumpkin spice everything" long before December rolls in.

And I get it. Sometimes, we just need Christmas to come early. These lyrics have been running through my head this entire Fall season,

For we need a little Christmas
Right this very minute

Candles in the window
Carols at the spinet
Yes, we need a little Christmas
Right this very minute...
For I've grown a little leaner
Grown a little colder
Grown a little sadder
Grown a little older...
Need a little Christmas now

Sometimes we need Christmas to come early. For some of us, this past year holds disappointments and losses and we are grieving. For some of us, loneliness, apathy, strained relationships, fear, and depression haunt the halls of our homes. The realities of life in a broken world weigh like a blanket of darkness on our souls.

It's tempting to think—what I need is for something really good to come my way. What I need is for God to heal that relationship. What I need is a better job. What I really need is a break from the pain and heaviness of this year. But that isn't what we really need.

What we really need is him. We need Jesus.

Advent reminds us that what we really need, we already have.

In my desperation, God came near. Despite my sin, in my despair, and even in my apathy, God comes near. And he comes personally to you and he comes personally to me.

He gives hope to the hopeless. Hope that doesn't come from a change in circumstances, but comes as a gift to a despairing heart that can no longer muster up any hope. He gives joy to the joyless. Joy that comes because the Gentle One draws near to the suffering and the hurting. He gives comfort. Comfort that comes from his very Presence which he freely offers to the one who ironically battles the despair of isolation and loneliness by withdrawing from everyone.

God came. And that's worth celebrating. So, let it come early! We all need a little Christmas.

Chapter Ninety-Nine
JOY AND SORROW

*For we do not have a high priest who is unable
to sympathize with our weakness, but one who in every
respect has been tempted as we are, yet without sin.*
Hebrews 4:15

The Christmas tree is a profound picture of the Advent season. It holds within it the tension of two realities that exist at the same time, two states that are simultaneously true.

On the one hand, Christmas trees are beautiful. Soft lights shimmer in the darkness, shiny ornaments sparkle and handmade treasures evoke precious memories. When presents surround the tree, hope and wonder abound.

Yet at the same time, the tree is dead.... or at least quickly dying. When you replace a fallen ornament, the branches are prickly and sharp. When the dog's wagging tail swats the limbs, dry needles instantly shower to the ground. A peek past the vibrant green exterior reveals a dry brown core.

This dual reality deeply comforts me. At a time when we celebrate the wonderful birth of our Savior, and you feel like you ought to (and perhaps even want to) be joyful and triumphant but you aren't, it is reassuring to know that this is the reality of Christmas.

Both actualities exist together. There is beauty and death, hope and loss, joy and pain. And Christ knows this well for his life encapsulated both.

There is joy.

*Fear not, for behold, I bring you **good news of great joy** that will be for all the people. For unto you is born this day in the city of David a Savior, who is Christ the Lord.* (Luke 2:10–11)

There is sorrow.

*He [Jesus] was despised and rejected by men, **a man of sorrows**, and acquainted with grief; and as one from whom men hide their faces he was despised, and we esteemed him not.* (Isaiah 53:3)

Knowing that Jesus not only understands that tension, but he himself experienced the reality of both emotions existing at the same time, is a sweet comfort to my soul.

Maybe your season has been similar in some ways to mine. Maybe you are wrestling with sorrow and joy. Maybe you feel both hope and disappointment. Maybe the weight of relational rejection is coupled with the embrace of the Father.

Know this—the One who has been born to us has been where you are. He experienced both too. You are free to wrestle in the tension of both truths. He is right with you. He is on your side. He will never leave you. He is Immanuel.

Chapter One Hundred
NOT A HALLMARK MOVIE

For to us a child is born, to us a son is given; and the government shall be upon his shoulder, and his name shall be called Wonderful Counselor, Mighty God, Everlasting Father, Prince of Peace.
Isaiah 9:6

'Tis the season of Christmas cookies, Christmas carols, and Christmas cards! Christmas lights. Christmas decorations. Christmas parties. I love it all!

But, despite all the wonderful delights the Advent season brings, often our lives don't look quite like the perfect Hallmark movies. For some of us, this Christmas season brings painful memories, unwelcome "firsts," the disappointment of unmet expectations, or the harsh reality of broken dreams. For some of us the season is so overwhelmingly busy with to-do lists galore that sitting and reflecting on the Coming of Jesus just doesn't make it onto our crowded calendar—and that makes us feel guilty.

If you fit into any of those camps, I have good news for you today! Our Savior has come! Because life in this world brings disappointment and brokenness, our Savior has come. Because sin and death have caused us deep pain and grief, our Savior has come. Because despite our best efforts, we still can't seem to get our priorities straight, our Savior has come.

And not only has he come, but he has come **to us**, to you. He invites us, broken and weak, struggling and failing, hurting and guilty, to come to him. He invites us, just as we are, to come to him. To be real. To be welcomed. To be loved.

That's why I love this Christmas card from my college roommate so much. I pull it out every year and smile. I love that one child is screaming and the other is miserable. I love that she and her husband are wearing grumpy faces under the word "Joy." I love it because it reminds me that Christmas is the time to be real.

Jesus invites us to be real. Sometimes we look around and it appears that everyone else's Christmas season is perfect and magical. Wrongly, we believe that we're the only ones who have holiday disappointments and hurts. But, that's just not reality. We all carry something. And that's the wonder of Christmas— **the One who has come invites us to come to him just as we are** —imperfect, broken, hurting, and weak.

So come to Him. Be real with Him. Just as you are. You are welcomed and wanted. Your Savior has come.

> *Come to me, all who labor and are heavy laden, and I will give you rest. Take my yoke upon you, and learn from me, for I am gentle and lowly in heart, and you will find rest for your souls. For my yoke is easy, and my burden is light.* (Matthew 11:28–30)

ABOUT THE AUTHOR

Judie Puckett serves as the Director of Spiritual Formation for Women at Chapelgate Presbyterian Church in Marriottsville, Maryland, and is currently working towards a Masters of Theology from Reformed Theological Seminary. In addition to serving at Chapelgate, Judie enjoys speaking at women's retreats and conferences.

Serving in ministry has been a part of Judie's story for over 25 years. She is passionate about connecting the mind and the heart —beautiful doctrine and ignited passion. She also believes the community of faith is one of God's greatest gifts to his people.

She and her husband have three wonderful children. Their family lives on a small farm where they raise cows and spoil their two dogs. She enjoys spending time with friends over a coffee or dessert, playing games, traveling and reading a good mystery.

To connect with Judie about speaking at your women's retreat or conference, contact her at GraceEnjoyed@outlook.com

ABOUT WHITE BLACKBIRD BOOKS

White blackbirds are extremely rare, but they are real. They are blackbirds that have turned white over the years as their feathers have come in and out over and over again. They are a redemptive picture of something you would never expect to see but that has slowly come into existence over time.

There is plenty of hurt and brokenness in the world. There is the hopelessness that comes in the midst of lost jobs, lost health, lost homes, lost marriages, lost children, lost parents, lost dreams, loss.

But there also are many white blackbirds. There are healed marriages, children who come home, friends who are reconciled. There are hurts healed, children fostered and adopted, communities restored. Some would call these events entirely natural, but really they are unexpected miracles.

The books in this series are not commentaries, nor are they crammed with unique insights. Rather, they are a collage of biblical truth applied to current times and places. The authors share their poverty and trust the Lord to use their words to strengthen and encourage his people.

May this series help you in your quest to know Christ as he is found in the Gospel through the Scriptures. May you look for and even expect the rare white blackbirds of God's redemption through Christ in your midst. May you be thankful when you look down and see your feathers have turned. May you also rejoice when you see that others have been unexpectedly transformed by Jesus.

ALSO BY WHITE BLACKBIRD BOOKS

A Year With the New Testament: A Verse By Verse Daily Devotional (2 Volumes)

All Are Welcome: Toward a Multi-Everything Church

The Almost Dancer

Birth of Joy: Philippians

Carrying Casseroles on Motorcycles

Choosing a Church: A Biblical and Practical Guide

Christ in the Time of Corona: Stories of Faith, Hope, and Love

Co-Laborers, Co-Heirs: A Family Conversation

The Crossroads of Adultery: A Journey of Repentance and Faith

Doing God's Work

Driven By Desire: Insatiable Longings, Incredible Promises, Infinite God

EmbRACE: A Biblical Study on Justice and Race

Ever Light and Dark: Telling Secrets, Telling the Truth

Everything Is Meaningless? Ecclesiastes

Faithful Doubt: Habakkuk

Grace-Centered Economics: A Biblical Theology of Economics

Heal Us Emmanuel: A Call for Racial Reconciliation, Representation, and Unity in the Church

Hear Us, Emmanuel: Another Call for Racial Reconciliation, Representation, and Unity in the Church

How to Speak a Sermon: So That People Will Listen

The Organized Pastor: Systems to Care for People Well

Our Heads on Straight: Sober-mindedness—A Forgotten Christian Virtue

Plunder: Unearthing Truth for Marketplace and Ministry Leadership

Questions of the Heart: Leaning In, Listening For, and Loving Well Toward True Identity in Christ

Rooted: The Apostles' Creed

Single-Handedly Blessed

A Sometimes Stumbling Life

To You I Lift Up My Soul: Confessions and Prayers

Urban Hinterlands: Planting the Gospel in Uncool Places

Follow storied.pub for titles and releases.

Made in the USA
Columbia, SC
02 December 2024

48305485R00141